Table of Contents

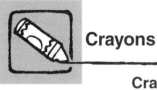 **Crayons**

Crayon Count 5
counting; number recognition; more or less

Which Go Together? 8
sorting objects into sets

My Favorite Color 11
making a graph

How Many Crayons in the Box? 15
adding sets together

Crayon Centers 17
patterning; sorting into sets; matching numbers; numerical order

 Frogs

Catch Flies for the Frogs 22
counting; number recognition; more or less

Frogs and Toads 25
sorting objects into sets; ordinal numbers

Touch a Frog 26
making a graph

Lilypad Hop 31
number recognition; numerical order; geometric shapes

Find My Lilypad 33
counting; number recognition; numerical order

Frog Centers 39
numerical order; counting; number recognition; patterning

 Buttons

Button Up My Jacket 43
counting; number recognition; more/same/less

Buttons, Buttons, Sort the Buttons 46
sorting objects into sets

How Many Buttons Are You Wearing? 49
making a graph

Button Centers 52
counting; number recognition; patterning; number match

Puppies

Feed the Puppies 56
counting; number recognition; number names, beginning addition

Sort the Puppies 61
sorting objects into sets

Which Puppy Do You Like Best? 67
making a graph

Follow the Puppy 71
number recognition; geometric shapes

Puppies in a Row 74
numerical order; ordinal numbers

Puppy Centers 76
counting; sorting into sets; patterning; numerical order

Mittens

How Many Mittens? 81
counting; number recognition; numerical order; counting by twos

Make a Pair 88
sorting into pairs; patterning

Do you Wear Mittens? 93
making a graph

Mitten Centers 96
number match; geometric shapes; patterning

Peanuts

Feed the Elephant 99
counting; number recognition

Sort the Shells 103
sorting into sets

How Many Nuts Are in Your Shell? 106
making a graph; counting

Peanut Centers 109
number match; number names; patterning

Preparation and Use of Games for Practicing Skills

Students are always eager to play games. During this play much learning takes place. While an identified skill such as sequencing numbers is practiced, students are also becoming better listeners and observers and are taking turns and cooperating in a group.

"Playing" with a small group gives a teacher the opportunity to closely observe students, to see their strengths, and assess where they need more help. It is also easier to provide immediate positive responses.

When to Use

Play a game whenever you have a group of students needing to practice one of the skills covered in the games (see the table of contents for a skill list).

Many of the games in this book can be played in five or ten minute periods. Use aides, parent volunteers, and cross-age tutors to play games with small groups.

The games can also be sent home to be played with a parent or siblings.

How to Use

Select the games that are appropriate for your students.

Prepare the playing pieces in advance — this is a great time to call on parent volunteers. Many parents who are unable to come during school hours may be willing to make a game for class if you send materials and directions home.

Using Math Games in Centers

Most of the games and game variations in this book can be played by a pair of students. Many can be played as a sorting or matching puzzle by one student once they have been taught to a group.

Follow these steps:

1. Make a copy of the playing pieces.

2. Color, cut out, and laminate the pieces.

3. Put the pieces in an envelope, a self-closing plastic bag, or an appropriately sized box with a lid.

4. Put a picture and the name of the game on the outside of the container.

5. Place the games on an accessible table or shelf.

Large games can be stored in a plastic or wire storage bin.

Small games can be stored in a shoe box or in the pockets of a hanging shoe bag or word card holder attached to a wall.

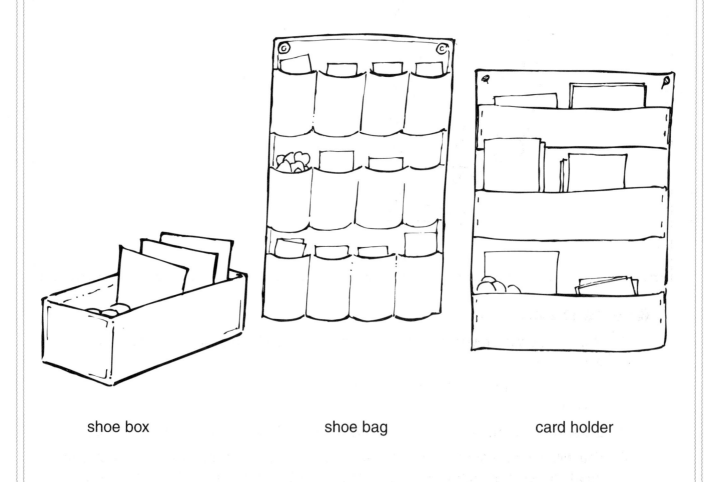

shoe box   shoe bag   card holder

Crayon Count

How to Make

1. Reproduce the crayon box counting card on page 7. You will need one card for each child.

2. Reproduce, laminate, and cut out one set of number cards (see inside back cover).

3. Determine the numerals to be practiced and put those cards in a small sack.

4. You will need a set of crayons for each child. Color is unimportant, but each child needs at least as many crayons as the largest number they will be practicing.

How to Play

1. Have students sit in a circle. Give each child a crayon box counting card and a set of crayons.

2. Pass the sack around so each child can pick a number.

3. Students read their numbers and put that many crayons "in the crayon box." Go around the circle having each child tell how many crayons are in their box. ("I have six crayons in my box.") If a child makes a mistake, have him/her touch each crayon and count in sequence.

4. Collect the number cards and pass the sack around again to continue play.

Play with Beginners

Call a child to come and sit with you. Place a number of crayons on a crayon box counting card. The child counts the crayons and puts the same amount next to the card. (If the child is not yet counting independently, have him/her place a crayon below each one on the card, and then touch and count the crayons with you.) Repeat this with each child in the group using a different number of crayons each time.

Variation—More or Less

Give each child a set of eight crayons. Lay out two crayons and ask "How many crayons do you see?" After students respond, say "Show me more than two crayons." Allow each child to tell how many crayons are in their sets of "more than two." Repeat several times and then ask students to show less than a given amount.

Play with Beginners

Lay out two crayons and have students tell how many they see. Then lay four crayons next to the two crayons. Ask "Which pile (set) is more?" Repeat several times with different numbers of crayons. Then follow the same process asking students to decide which is less. (You may need to practice "more" in one session and "less" in another session.)

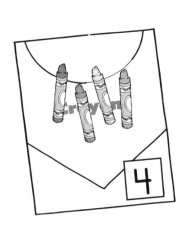 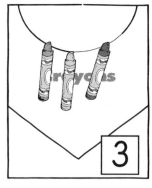 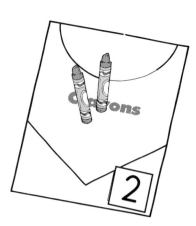

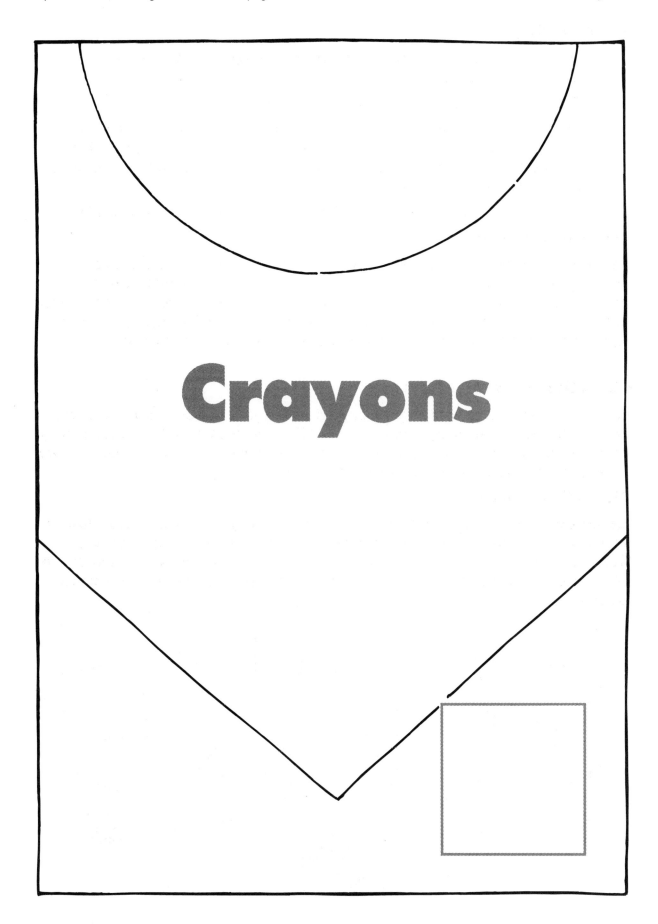

Crayons

Which Go Together?

How to Make

Provide an assortment of six to eight crayons — some with paper, some without paper, some whole, some broken pieces — for each child doing the activity. Reproduce the sorting sheets on page 10 to use with this activity.

How to Play

1. Students sit in a circle with the teacher. Give each student two or more sorting sheets and a pile of assorted crayons.

2. Ask students to sort the crayons by color. Ask, "How did you sort the crayons?" Have them remove the crayons from their sorting sheets.

3. Next have them sort the crayons by size. Again have them explain how the crayons have been sorted. Remove the crayons once more and have them sorted by covering (paper/no paper).

4. Ask students to think of other ways the crayons can be sorted (points/no points; flat/round; old/new; etc.).

Play with Beginners

Have students find all of the crayons sharing one attribute. For example:

- Find all of the red crayons.
- Find all of the broken crayons.
- Find all of the crayons in paper.

Advanced Play

Have students sort the crayons into piles (sets) by two attributes. For example, a child might sort the crayons in one of these ways:

- red wrapped crayons
- red unwrapped crayons
- broken crayons with paper
- broken crayons without paper
- whole crayons with paper
- whole crayons without paper

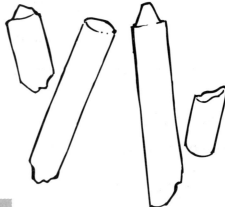

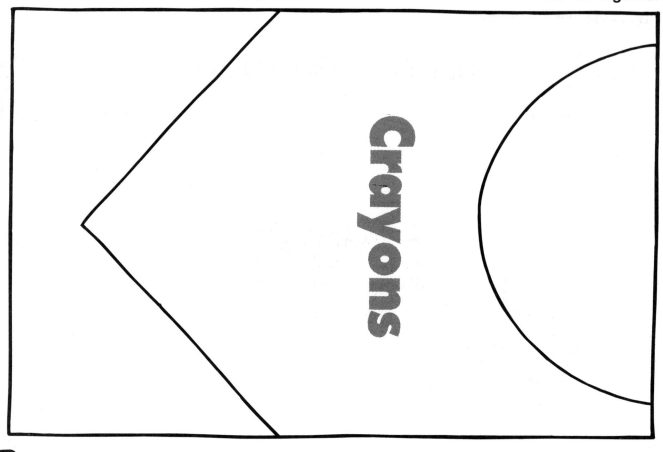

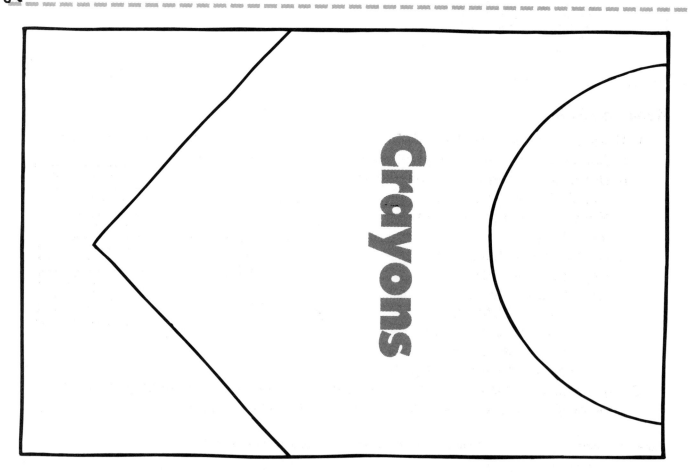

My Favorite Color

How to Make

1. Make a graph following these directions. (This graph is meant to be placed on the floor.)
   a. Cut a 6-foot (2 meter) length of 36" (1 meter) wide butcher paper.
   b. Use a marking pen to divide the graph into 6" (16.5 cm) squares). You will make a graph with six columns of 12 boxes.
   c. Reproduce the header card on page 13 on tagboard. (Use as few as two cards or as many as six with this activity.) Color and cut out the cards. Fold each card in half. Sit the cards in a row along one end of the graph.

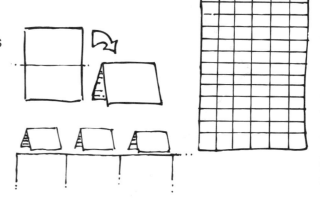

2. Have available at least one crayon of each color represented on the graph for each child playing the game. Place the crayons in a small box or sack.

Note: This same graph form can be used for other graphs by changing the header cards.

How to Play

1. Have students sit around the graph.

2. Have each child pick their favorite color from the crayons you have provided.

3. Ask each child to name the color chosen and place it on the graph. Child says, "Yellow is my favorite color. I am putting it in the yellow row."

4. When all students have placed their crayon on the graph, ask questions such as the following:

> • What can we find out from this graph?
>
> • Which has the most? Which has the least?
>
> • Are there any rows (columns) that are the same?
>
> • How many _____ are there?
>
> • Are there more (less) _____ or _____ ?

Advanced Play

1. Make a wall graph on a sheet of butcher paper (6' x 36" [2 m x 1 m]). Divide the paper into 6" (16.5cm) columns. Draw a line 6" (16.5cm) from the top.

2. Reproduce the crayon patterns on page 14. You will need one crayon for each student and for each of the six heading boxes.

3. Color six crayons and glue them in the heading boxes. Write in the color words if appropriate to the level of your students.

4. Give one crayon pattern to each child. Each child picks his/her favorite color from the six represented on the graph and colors his/her crayon that color. Repeat steps 3 and 4 on page 11 with students gluing their crayon in the correct column on the wall graph.

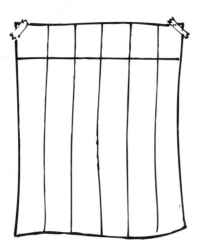

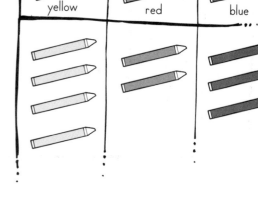

fold

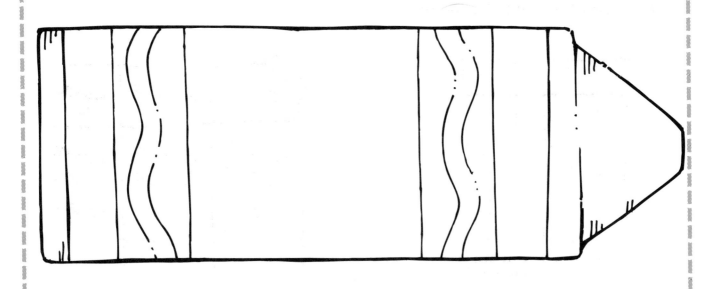

Note: Reproduce the crayon patterns to use with the wall graph on page 12.

Pattern for My Favorite Color

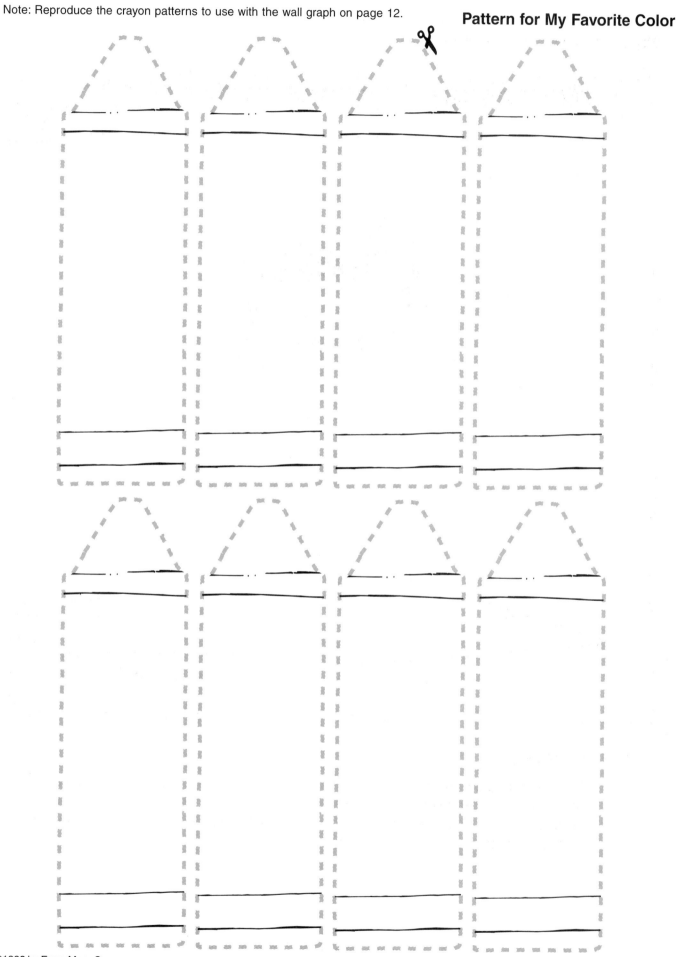

14

How Many Crayons in the Box?

How to Make

1. Cut crayons (see pattern page 14) from two colors of construction paper. Make a crayon set for each child playing the game.
2. Make the outline of a "crayon box" on the floor with masking tape or yarn. It needs to be large enough for several students to stand inside.

How to Play

1. Students sit around the "crayon box." Each child has one colored crayon.

2. Tap (or point to) two students with the same color crayon. Those two students step into the box. Teacher asks, "How many green crayons are in the box?"

3. Tap one child with the second color crayon. That child steps into the box. Ask, "How many yellow crayons in the box?" After students answer ask, "How many crayons are in the box all together?"

4. Once students agree on the number of crayons in the box, review the problem by saying, "Two green crayons and one yellow crayon make three crayons in all."

5. Repeat the process several more times.

Play with Beginners

Touch each child standing in the box and count. Students repeat the number as they count along.

Advanced Play

Write the numbers on the chalkboard as each problem is solved so students can see the equation.

Crayon Centers

• Crayon Patterns

Provide a supply of crayons and several patterning strips (see pages 20 and 21). The child's task is to select a strip and copy the pattern using real crayons.

For more advanced students, provide crayons cut from construction paper in several colors (use a crayon from one of the strips on page 20 for a pattern) and blank strips of paper (4" x 12" [10 x 30.5 cm]). The child's task is to create a pattern with the paper crayons, and then to glue the pattern to the paper strip.

• Sort the Colors

Create a center sorting activity by providing a box of broken crayons along with a set of containers each labeled with a different color. (Glue a colored paper "crayon" to the outside of the container, wrap the container in colored construction paper, or, if students are ready, write the name of the color on the can.)The child's task is to sort all of the crayons into their correct containers.

• Number Match

Reproduce the crayons on pages 18 and 19. Color, laminate, and cut out the pieces. The child's task is to match each number to the correct set of dots.

• Numerical Order

Use the crayons containing numbers from Number Match to practice sequencing numbers. The child's task is to arrange the numbered crayons in order beginning with 1 (or the smallest number represented).

Note: Reproduce the crayons to use with the center game on page 17.

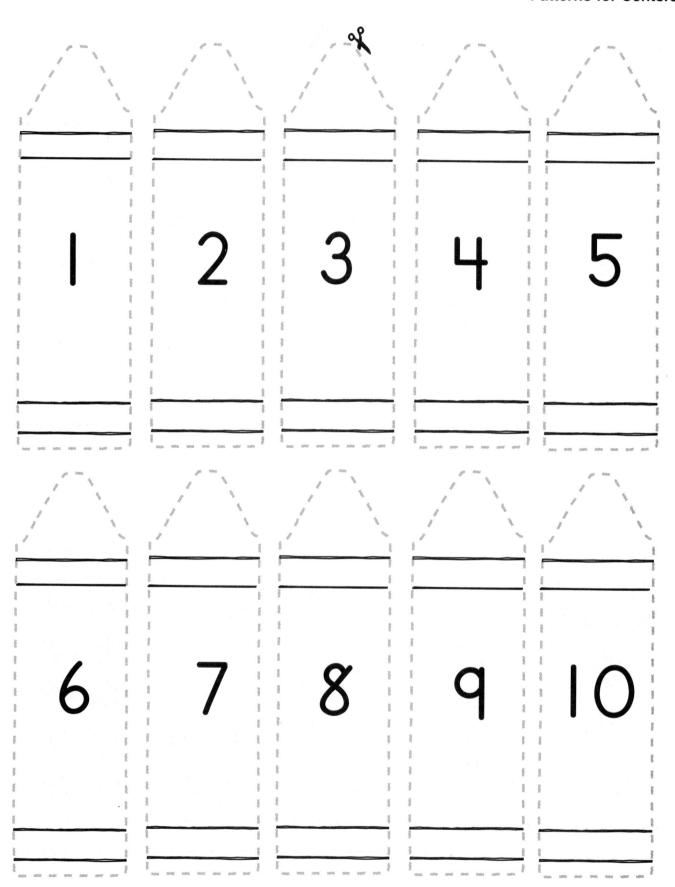

Note: Reproduce the crayons to use with the center game on page 17.

Patterns for Centers

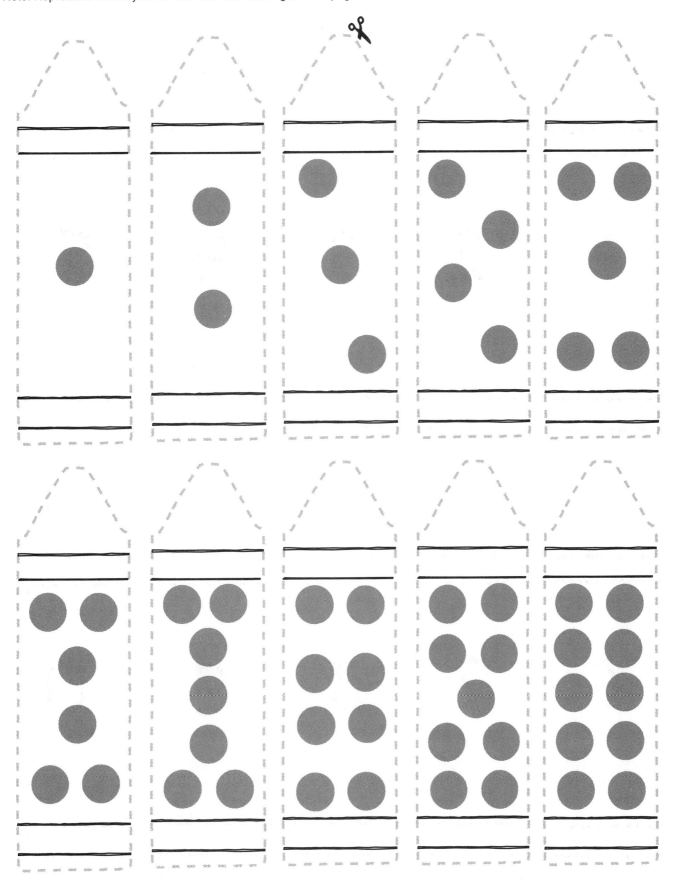

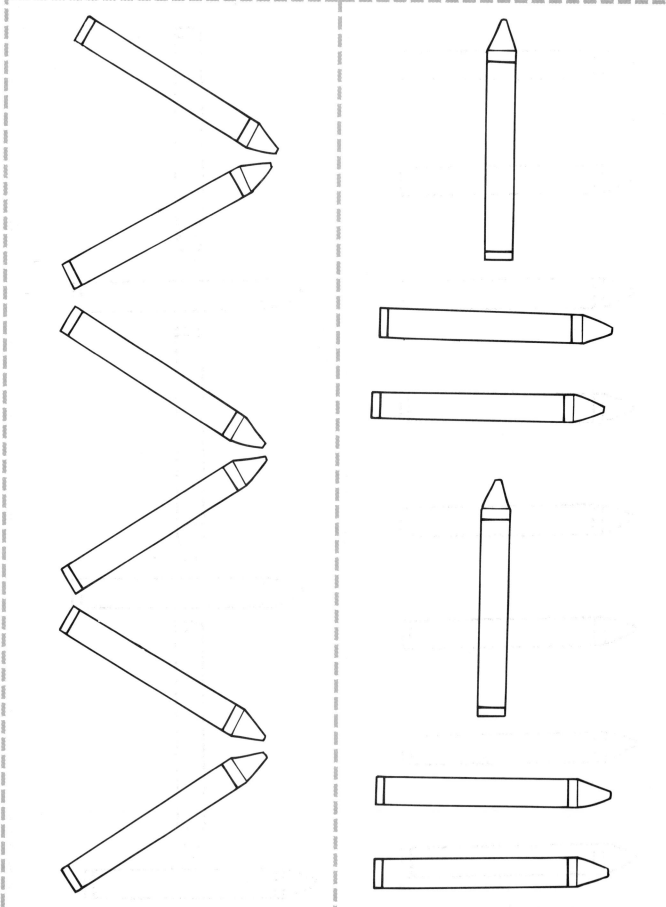

Note: Reproduce the crayon patterning cards to use with the center on page 17. **Patterns for Centers**

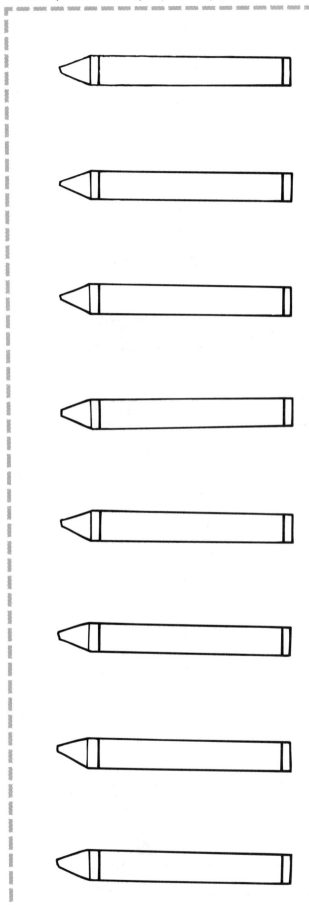

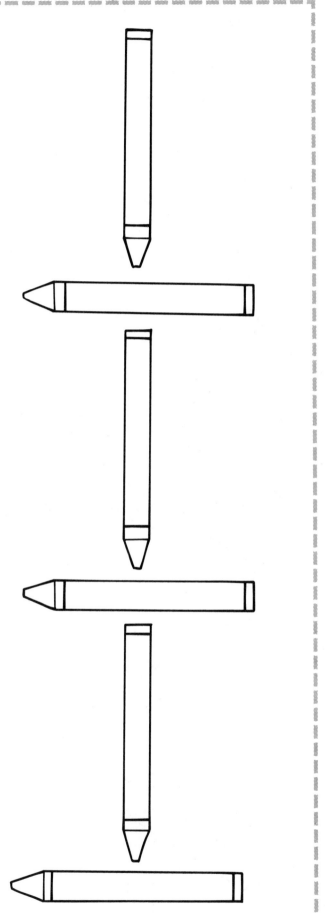

Catch Flies for the Frogs

How to Make

1. Use a large sheet of posterboard to create a playing board. Divide the board into six sections.

2. Reproduce the large fly on page 24 six times.

3. Color and cut out the flies. Write the numbers 0 to 5 on the flies. Glue one fly in each box in the order shown.

4. Draw a frog using green permanent marker on a beanbag. If you do not have a beanbag, fill a small green sock with beans, tie off the end tightly with string or yarn, and draw eyes and a mouth on it with black permanent marking pen.

5. Purchase small plastic flies at a party supply shop or reproduce several sheets of the small flies on page 24. Cut the flies apart and put into a self-closing plastic bag for storage.

6. Draw a green frog in the middle of a small paper plate (or use the pattern on page 27). You will need one plate for each player.

How to Play

1. Tape the playing board to the floor. Put a strip of masking tape several steps away from the board to mark where the player will stand. (The distance will depend on the age and motor development of your students.)

2. Each player stands behind the masking tape marker and throws the beanbag at the board to "catch flies."

3. Have the player read the number the bean bag lands on. The player then counts out that many flies from the storage bag and places them on his/her frog plate.

4. After each child has had a turn, go around the group and ask each child to tell how many flies the frog has eaten.

5. Continue play until each child has had several turns. Repeat steps 3 and 4 each time.

Advanced Play—Same, More or Less

As each child plays ask "Does anyone have the same number of flies as (child's name)?" "Does anyone have more flies?" "Does anyone have less/not as many flies?"

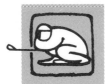

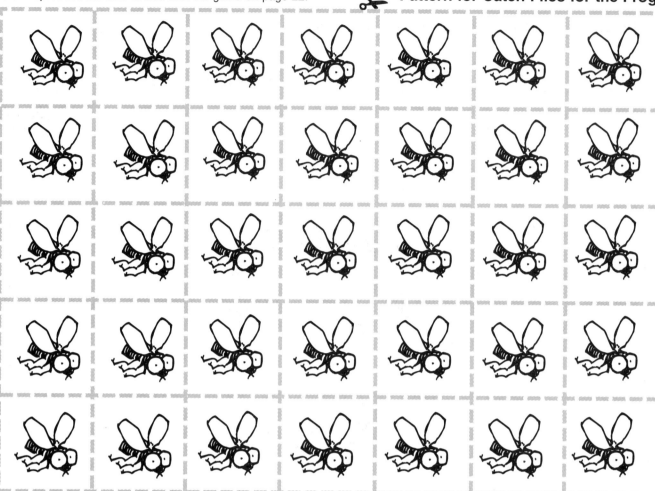

Frogs and Toads

How to Make

1. Reproduce the frogs on page 27 on green construction paper. Reproduce the toads on page 28 on brown construction paper.

2. Laminate and cut out the frogs and toads.

3. Place them in a small sack or box.

How to Play

1. Have students sit in a circle with the teacher.

2. Keep one frog and one toad. Pass the sack around and have each child take one piece.

3. Place a frog in the center of the circle and a toad in another spot in the center. Point to the frog and "This is a frog. If you have a frog put it here." Then point to the toad and say "This is a toad. If you have a toad put it here."

4. Collect the frogs and toads. Play again sorting in a new way:

- size
- sitting or jumping
- bumpy or smooth

Variation—Ordinal Numbers

Have students sit in a line facing the teacher. Begin with only three frogs or toads. Use those with distinctive differences so students will have no difficulty describing them (for example: small hopping frog, large sitting toad, small sitting frog). Ask "Which one is first in line? Which is last in line?" Remove the last one and ask "Which one is last now?"

Place several frogs and toads in a row. Have students repeat after you as you point to the frogs and toads and count "first, second, third, etc." Then ask questions such as:

- Which frog is second?
- Is the small bumpy toad first or last?
- Which frog is in third place—the little one or the big one?

Note: Reproduce the pictures to use with the game on page 25.

Patterns for Frog and Toad

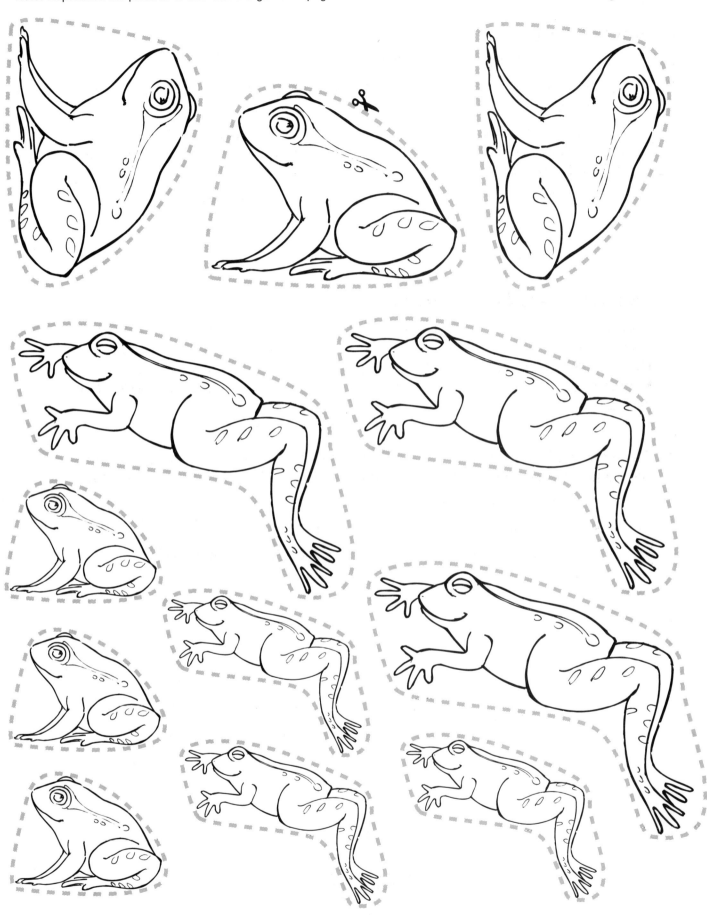

27

Note: Reproduce the pictures to use with the game on page 25.

Patterns for Frog and Toad

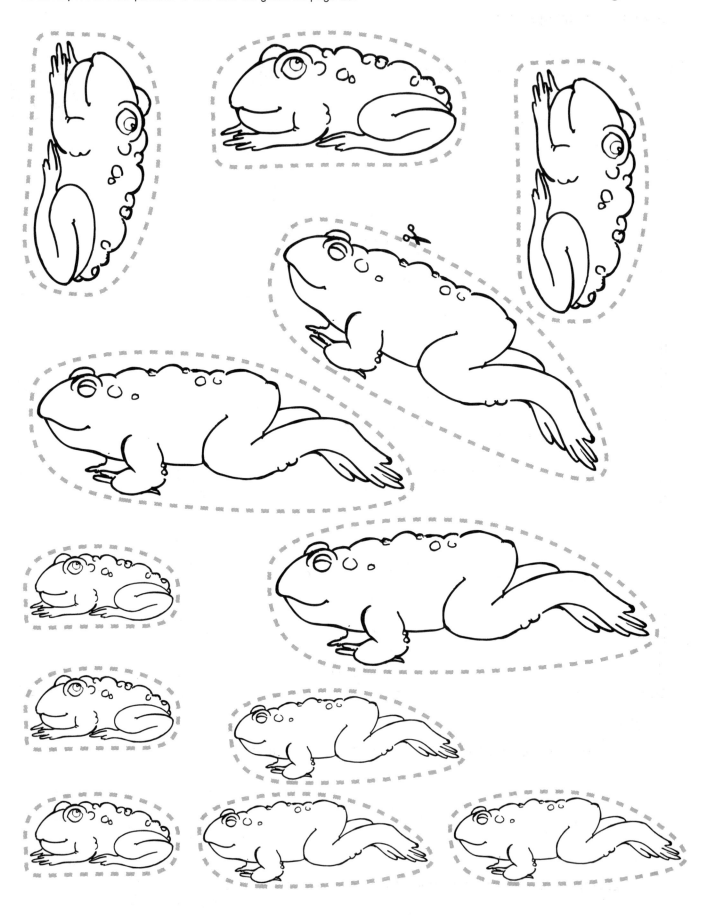

Touch a Frog

How to Make

1. Take a sheet of chart paper. Divide and label it as shown here.

   I have touched a frog.

2. Reproduce a frog pattern for each child (see page 27).

How to Play

1. Have the group playing the game sit with the teacher.

2. Talk about frogs, allowing students to explain when and where they have seen frogs up close.

3. Pass out a frog to each child. Have them write their names on the frogs (or have the names on them already for students who are at a prewriting level).

4. Tape a frog with your name on it to the graph and say, "I am putting my frog under 'yes' because I have touched a frog." Ask each child, one at a time, "Have you ever touched a frog?" Help the child tape his/her frog in the correct column on the graph. Have the child explain why the frog is going in that particular column.

5. When everyone has had a turn, ask questions such as:

    • How many people have touched a frog?

    • How many people have not touched a frog?

    • Which has more frogs — yes or no?

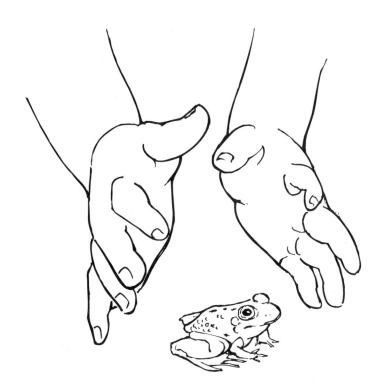

Lily Pad Hop

How to Make

1. Laminate a large sheet of green butcher paper. Cut it into 9" (23 cm) squares.

2. Cut large lily pads from the green squares. (Cut one lily pad for each number you wish to practice.)

3. Write a number on each lily pad with a permanent marking pen. (This game shows the numbers 1 - 10. You can use any sequence that is appropriate for your students.)

How to Play

1. Use masking tape to create a large "pond" on the floor. Tape the lily pads in the pond. Arrange them as shown here. Place them close enough together that students can hop from one to another.

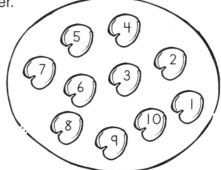

2. Students playing the game line up by the lily pad containing number 1.

3. One child at a time hops from lily pad to lily pad (in numerical order) and reads each number before landing on it. If a child reaches a point where he/she misreads a number or doesn't know where to go, give the number, and have the child continue. You may want students who make a mistake to return to the end of the line and have a second try.

   Students who make no errors sit around the outside of the pond until everyone has had a turn.

Note: Some young students may need to hold the teacher's hand while hopping.

Variation—Name the Shapes

Reproduce the shapes on page 112. Cut a set of lily pads and glue a shape to each one. Arrange the lily pads in a loose circle in the "pond." Ask students to hop from lily pad to lily pad, naming the shape before landing on it.

Advanced Play

Have students name the shape and then give one of its characteristics ("This is a triangle. It has three sides.").

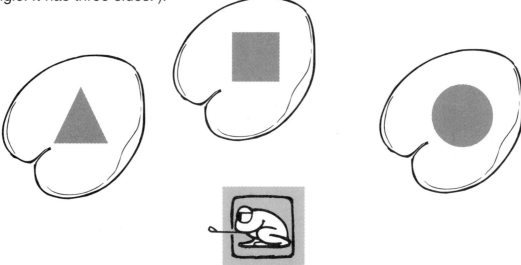

Find My Lily Pad

How to Make

1. Reproduce the frogs and lily pads on pages 35 - 38.

2. Laminate and cut out the playing pieces.

How to Play

1. Have students sit in a circle with the teacher.

2. Pass out the lily pads to the players.

3. Show one frog at a time and ask "Can you find my lily pad?" Students count the flies on their lily pads. The child with the lily pad matching the number on the frog lays it in the center of the circle. Place the frog on the lily pad. Encourage players to say why they are putting the lily pad down. ("The lily pad has one fly. It belongs to the '1' frog.")

4. Continue until all frogs and lily pads have been matched.

Play with Beginners

Lay down all of the lily pads in a row. Hold one frog next to each lily pad and ask, "I am frog six. Is this my lilypad?" Continue down the row until the group agrees that a frog and lily pad match. Put the frog on the lily pad. Continue until all frogs are matched to their lilypads.

Variation—Frogs Parade

Use only the frogs to practice number sequence. Pass out all the frogs except "1" to the players. Place "1" in the center of the circle. Have the students place their frogs in the correct order after the "1."

When all numbers are in order, have the group read the numbers aloud as you point to each number.

If your students are ready to practice sequencing farther, cover up the numbers on the frogs before reproducing the page. Write in additional numbers, laminate, and cut out the frogs.

Note: Reproduce the frogs to use with the game on page 33.

36

Note: Reproduce the lilypads to use with the game on page 33.

Patterns for Find My Lily Pad

Note: Reproduce the lilypads to use with the game on page 33.

Patterns for Find My Lily Pad

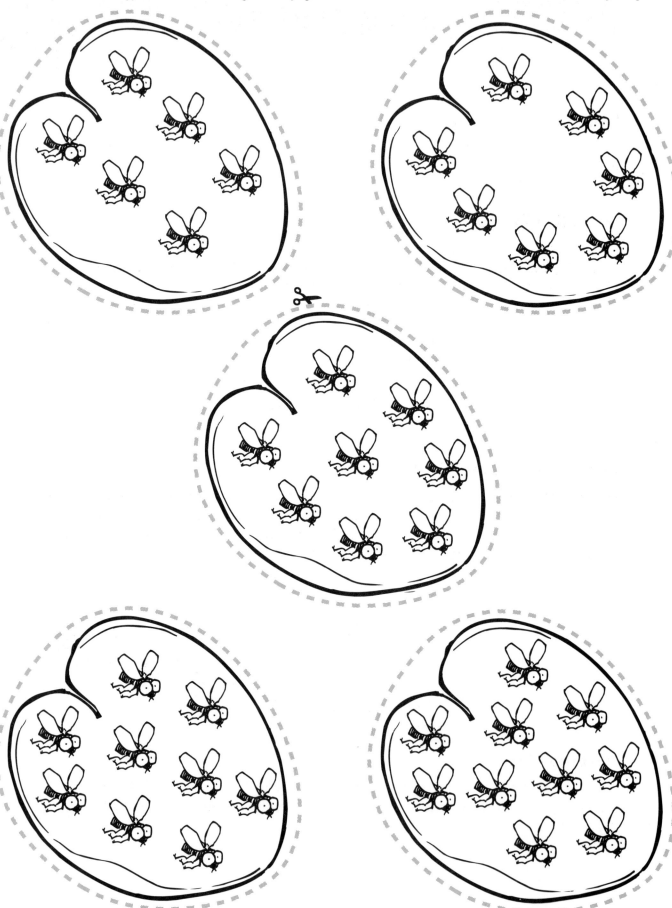

Frog Centers

• Sequence numbers

Put the frogs containing numbers (pages 35 and 36) in an envelope. The child's task is to put the frogs in order.

• Feed the Frogs

Make a frog plate (see page 23) for each number to be practiced. Write a number on each plate. Put a container of "flies" in the center along with the frog plates. The child's task is to read the number and put that amount of flies on the plate.

• Frog and Toad Patterns

Reproduce the patterning strips on page 40 and 41 and the frog and toad pictures on page 42. Color, laminate, and cut out the strips and frog and toad pieces (the colors on the patterning strips and the frogs and toads must be the same). The child's task is to match the pattern shown on the patterning strip.

Advanced Play

Provide a supply of frogs and toads and blank strips of paper (4" x 12" [10 x 30.5 cm]). The child's task is to create a pattern and then glue it to the blank paper strip.

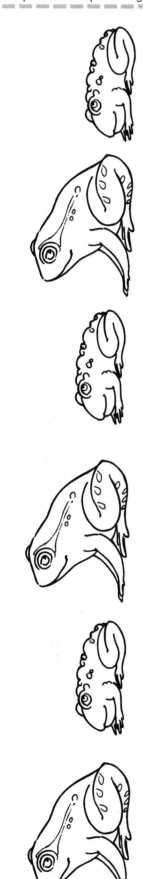

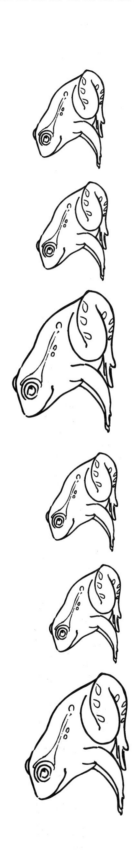

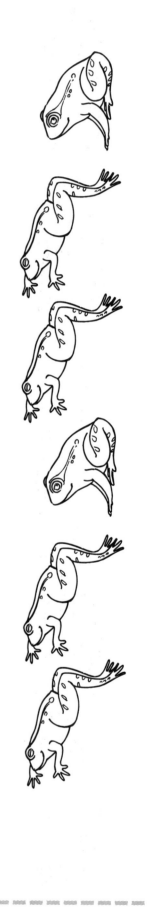

Math Games and Centers EMC 735

Patterns for Frog Centers

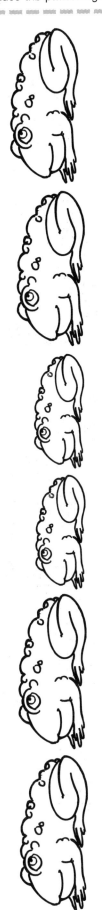

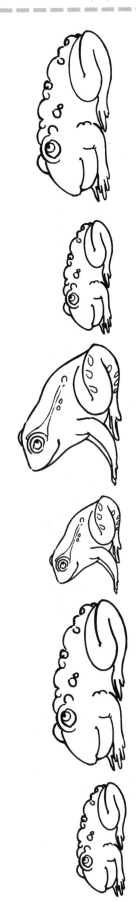

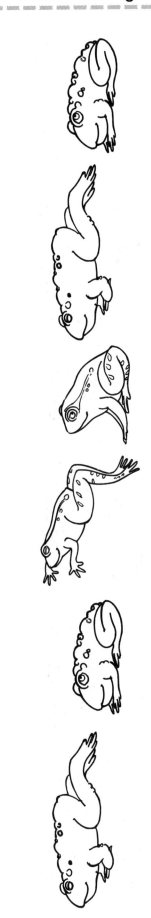

41

Patterns for Frog Centers

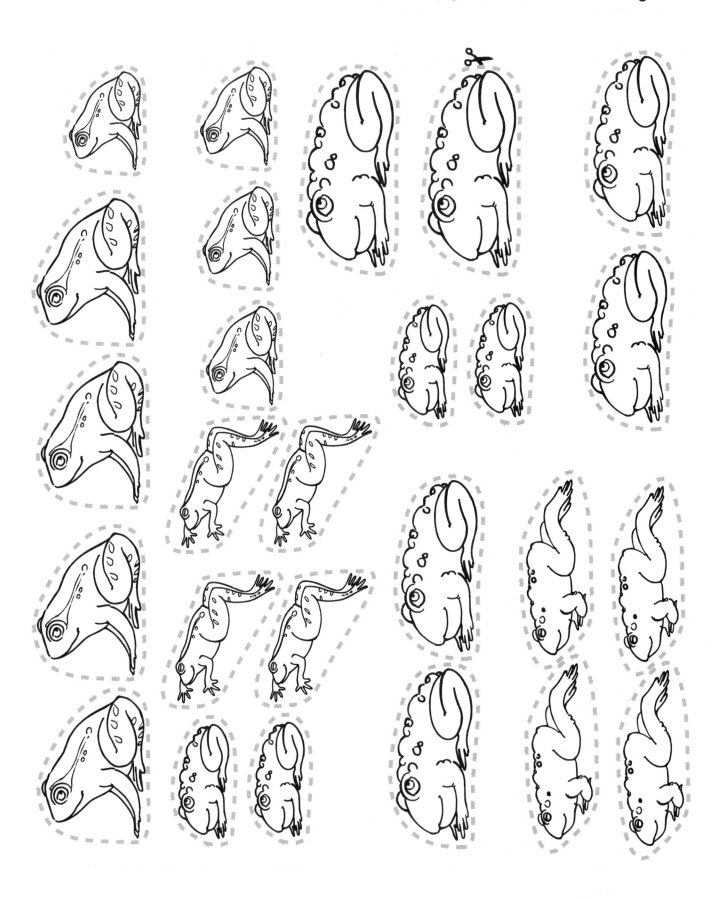

Math Games and Centers EMC 735

Button Up My Jacket

Note: Use small objects such as buttons only with close adult supervision. If you feel your students are not ready to use such small objects, cut large buttons from posterboard.

How to Make

1. Reproduce the soldier button - counting card on page 45 for each child and the number cards on the inside back cover.

2. Color and laminate the soldier counting cards.

3. Cut out the number cards.

4. Each child will need a handful of buttons equal to the largest number you intend to practice.

How to Play

1. Students sit in a circle with their counting card and buttons.

2. Pass out a number card to each child. Students lay the number card in the corner of their counting card, read the number, and place that many buttons on the soldier's coat. Have each child read their number and count their buttons aloud to the group.

3. Have students pass the number card to the right and repeat the process. Continue play until each child has practiced each number.

Advanced Play

Give each child a set of number cards, a counting card for each number, and a large supply of buttons. Have students lay out all of their cards, place a number card on each, and count out the correct number of buttons for each card.

Variation—More/Same/Less

Give each child a set of buttons. Lay out three buttons and ask "How many buttons do you see?" After students respond, say "Show me more than three buttons." Allow each child to tell how many buttons are in their sets of "more than three." Repeat several times and then ask students to show less than a given amount.

Play with Beginners

Lay out three buttons and have students tell how many they see. Ask them to lay out the same number of buttons. Repeat several times with different amounts.

Lay out two buttons and have students tell how many they see. Then lay five buttons next to the two buttons. Ask "Which pile (set) is more?" Repeat several times with different numbers of buttons. Then follow the same process, asking students to decide which is less. (You may need to do more and less at different sessions.)

Note: Reproduce the counting card to use with page 43.

Pattern for Button Up My Jacket

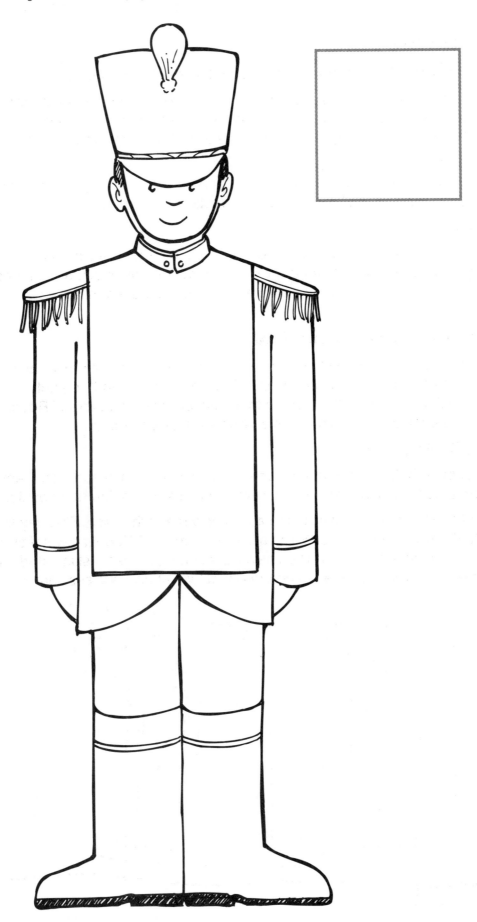

 Math Games and Centers EMC 735

Buttons, Buttons, Sort the Buttons

How to Make

Reproduce the button-sorting sheet on page 48 for each child. Provide buttons of different colors, sizes, shapes, and with different numbers of holes.

For students too young to use real buttons, draw large buttons on colored posterboard (circles, squares, and triangles in various colors and sizes). Laminate and cut out the buttons. Use these to sort by color, size, and shape.

How to Play

1. Have students sit in a circle. Provide each with a container of assorted buttons.

2. Discuss the various colors of buttons students have in their containers.

3. Have students sort their buttons into piles (sets) by color on their sorting sheets. When the sorting has been completed, ask questions such as:

    • Why did you put this button here?

    • How are all the buttons in this pile (set) the same?

    • What is your sorting rule?

    • What can you call this pile (set)?

    (Show a button) Does this button go in this pile (set)? Why?

4. Have students put the buttons back into their containers. Give a new sorting challenge (size, shape, number of holes, smooth/rough, plastic/wood/metal/glass).

Play with Beginners

Put a button in the center of the circle. Say "This button is red." Ask students to find a button with the same color (or other characteristic) in their button container.

Advanced Play

Ask students to sort according to more than one attribute. For example:

    • small, red buttons

    • large buttons with four holes

    • square plastic buttons

Note: Reproduce the sorting card to use with page 46.

Pattern for Buttons, Buttons Sort the Buttons

How Many Buttons Are You Wearing?

How to Make

1. Make a wall graph on a sheet of butcher paper (6' x 36" [2 m x 1 m]). Divide the paper into 6" (16.5 cm) columns. Draw a line 6" (16.5 cm) from the top.

2. Reproduce the button patterns (see page 51). You will need one button for each of the six heading boxes, and for each child.

3. Write a number in each heading box (0, 1, 2, 3, 4, 5 or more). Glue a button in the box.

With Beginners

Make a floor graph.

1. Use masking tape to create six rows wide enough for children to stand in.

2. Fold six sheets of 9" x 12" (23 x 30.5 cm) sheets of construction paper or tagboard in half. Write a number (0, 1, 2,3, 4, 5 or more) on each card. Glue an appropriate number of buttons in the box. Set one header at the end of each row.

How to Play

1. Give each child a button pattern.

2. Have students count the buttons they are wearing. (Encourage students to help each other.)

3. Students paste their buttons in the correct row on the wall graph.

4. When the graph is complete ask questions such as:

   - What can we find out from this graph?

   - Which column has the most? Which has the least?

   - Are there any rows (columns) that are the same? What does that tell us?

   - How many children had (three buttons)?

   - Did more children have (no buttons) or (five buttons) ?

Play with Beginners

1. Have students sit around the floor graph. Have each child count the number of buttons he/she is wearing. (Have students help each other as necessary.)

2. Have students form lines after the header card that correspond to their number of buttons on the floor graph.

3. Ask questions about what the graph shows.

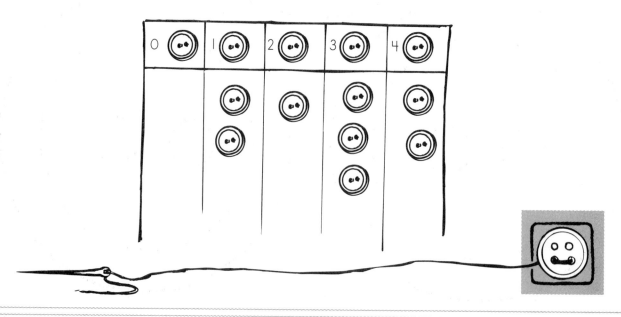

**Patterns for How Many Buttons
Are You Wearing?**

Math Games and Centers EMC 735

•Button Count

Write numbers on several plastic cups with a permanent marking pen. Place the cups and a container of buttons in the center. The child's task is to read each number and put that many buttons in the cup.

•Button Patterning

Provide patterning strips (see page 53) and a container of buttons (or buttons cut from posterboard). The child's task is to copy each of the patterns.

Extend the activity for more advanced students by providing blank strips of tagboard and a box of buttons. The student creates an original button pattern, and then glues the buttons to a tagboard strip (2" x 12" [5 x 30.5 cm]). Students leave their patterns at the center for others to duplicate.

•Button Puzzles

Reproduce the puzzle forms on pages 54 and 55. Color, laminate, and cut the pieces in half. The child's task is to match each number piece to its equivalent dot piece to complete the button puzzle.

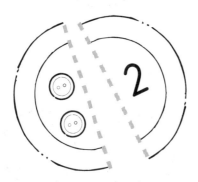
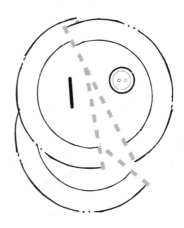

Patterns for Button Centers

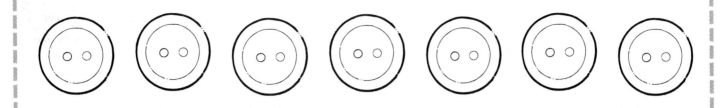

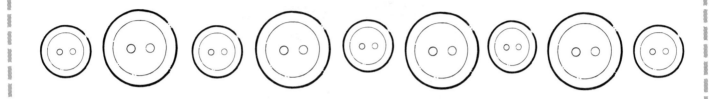

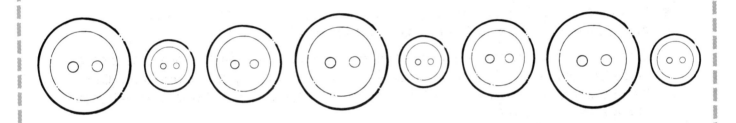

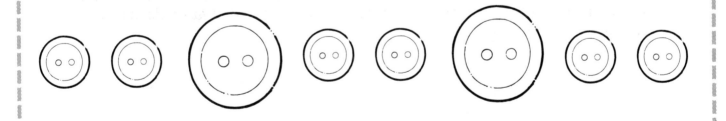

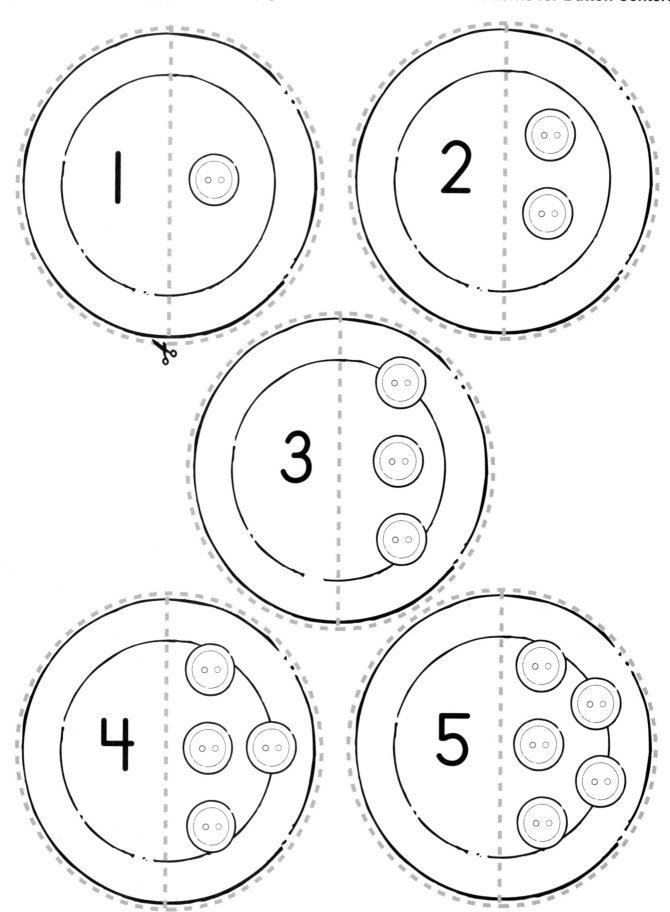

Patterns for Button Centers

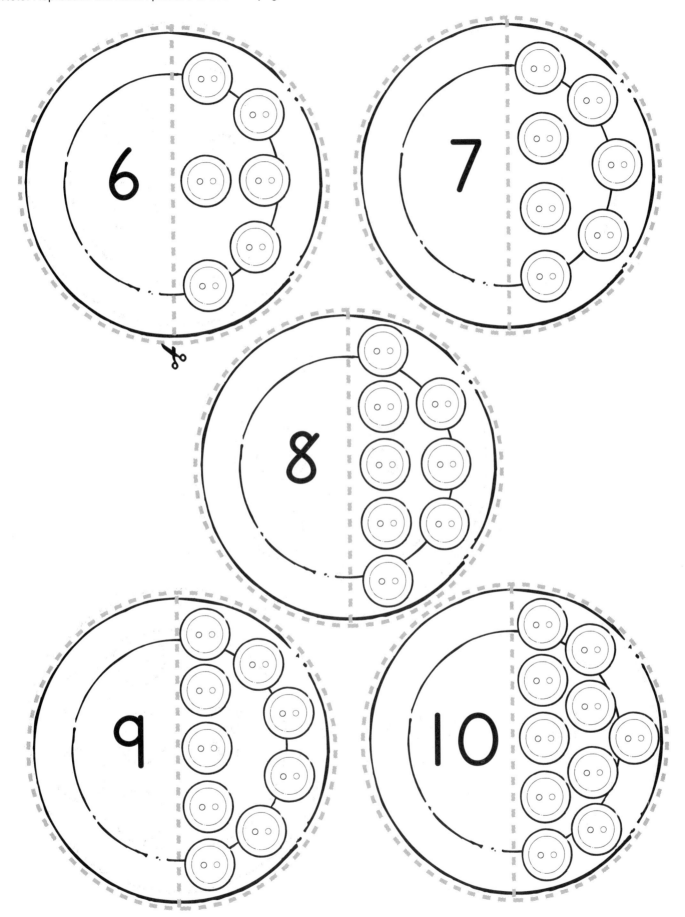

55

Feed the Puppies

How to Make

1. Reproduce the bowl counting cards on page 59.

2. Reproduce the bones on page 60. Make enough for each child to have as many as the largest number to be practiced.

3. Reproduce the number cards on the inside back cover.

4. Color, laminate, and cut out all playing pieces.

5. Put the number cards in a small sack.

Note: You may choose to use real bowls and dog bones.

How to Play

1. Have students sit in a circle. Give each child a food dish counting card and a set of bones.

2. Have each child pick a number from the sack.

3. Students read their number and put that many bones in the bowl. Go around the circle having each child tell how many bones are in the bowl. ("I put six bones in my puppy's bowl.") If a child makes a mistake, have him/her touch each bone and count in sequence.

4. Collect the number cards and pass the sack around again. Continue play.

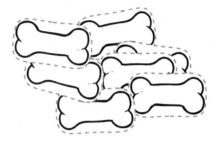

Play with Beginners

Call a child to come and sit with you. Place a number card on the counting card. The child counts out the correct number of bones. (If the child is not yet counting independently, have him/her place a bone below each one on the card, and then touch and count the bones with you.) Repeat this for each card.

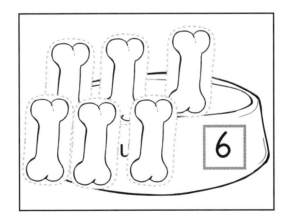

Variations

Number Match

Use the pattern on page 60 to make two sets of bones. Write numbers on one set of bones and sets of dots on the other bones. Pass out the bones containing numbers to students playing the game. Lay the bones containing dots in a row. Ask students one at a time to place their bone under the matching bone in the row.

Very Advanced Play

Put numbers on one set of bones and number words on a second set. Play following the directions in Number Match.

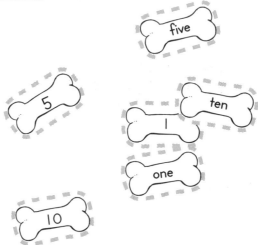

Beginning Addition

Reproduce a puppy food dish for each child playing the game. Cut bones from brown and white construction paper. Give each child a food dish and three bones of each color.

Have students put one brown bone in the food dish. Ask "How many brown bones did you put in the food dish?" Have them put one white bone in the food dish. Ask "How many white bones did you put in the food dish?" Then ask "How many bones are in the food dish?" (With more advanced students you can write the number sentence on a sentence strip to show and read with the students after they have given the answer.)

Repeat several times using different combinations of bones appropriate to the children's level.

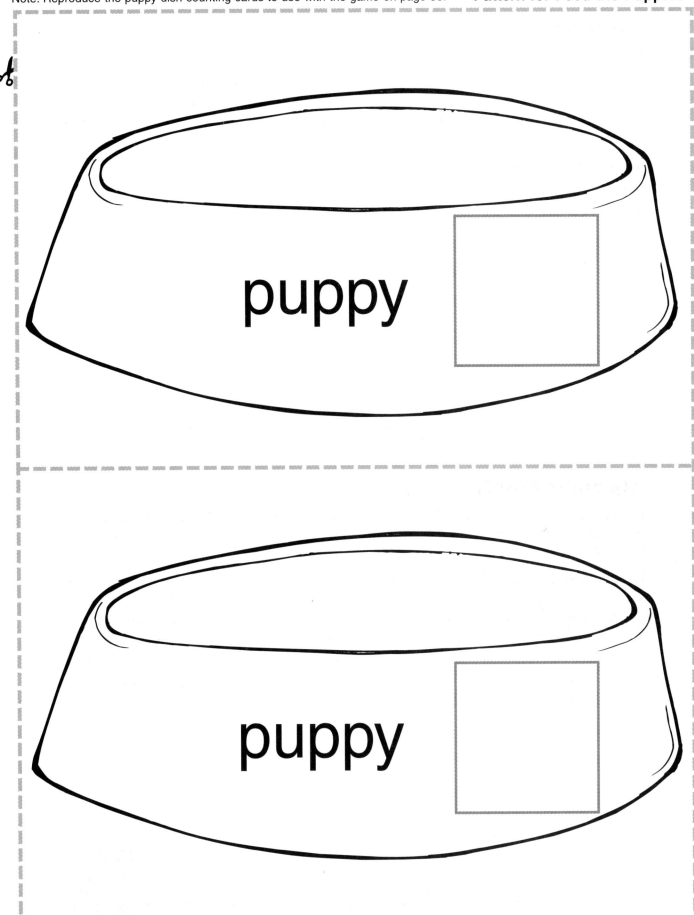

Note: Reproduce the dog bones to use with the game on page 56.

Patterns for Feed the Puppies

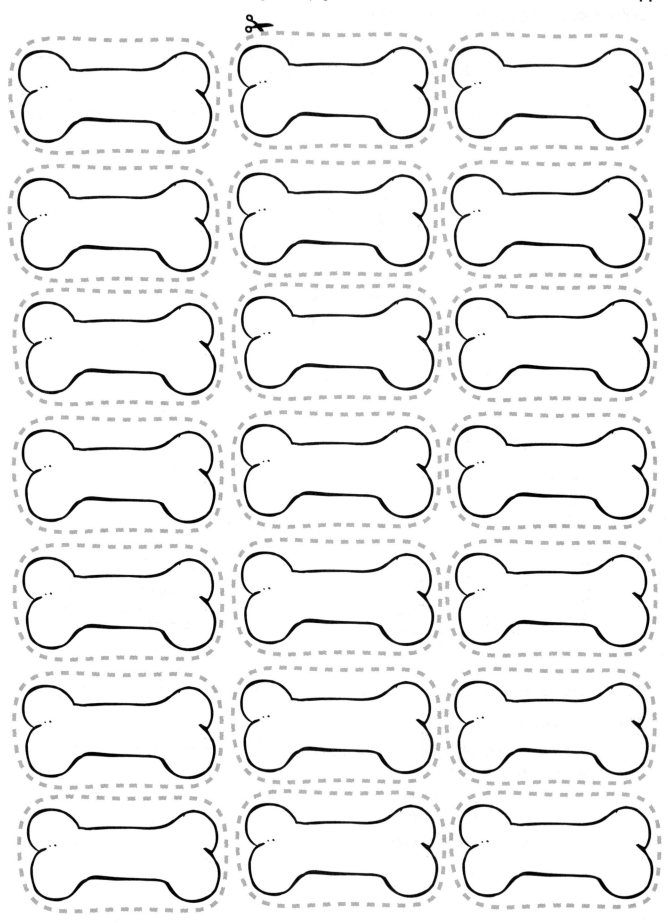

Math Games and Centers EMC 735

Sort the Puppies

How to Make

1. Bring in a number of stuffed dogs that can be sorted by various attributes (size, color, decoration, etc.).

2. Reproduce the puppies on pages 63 and 64. For advanced play, reproduce the mother dogs on pages 65 and 66.

3. Laminate and cut out the puppies.

How to Play

1. Have students sit in a circle. Introduce the lesson using stuffed toy dogs. Put the stuffed dogs in a pile in the middle of the circle. Ask students to separate the dogs into two sets—one for big dogs and one for small dogs.

   Return the dogs to one pile and give a new sorting direction (color, texture, ribbon/no ribbon, etc.). You may want to stop at this point with beginning learners.

3. Give each child one each of the eight types of puppy playing pieces. Discuss the ways the puppies are different (spots/no spots; long/short tail; ears up/ears down).

4. Ask students to sort their puppies with the spotted puppies in one pile and the puppies with no spots in the other pile. When the sorting has been completed, ask questions such as:

   Why did you put this puppy here?

   How are all the puppies in this pile (set) the same?

   (Show a puppy) Does this puppy go in this pile (set)? Why?

   What is your sorting rule?

   What can you call this pile (set)?

5. Give a new sorting challenge (length of hair, way ears go).

Play with Beginners

Put one puppy in the center of the circle and say "This puppy has spots. Do you have a puppy with spots?" Students lay any puppies with spots next to your puppy. Have students say "This puppy has spots" as they lay their puppies down.

Advanced Play

Lay out the four mother dogs. Say "These dogs have lost their puppies. Can you find them?" Ask students to put their puppies by the correct mother dog and then explain how they knew which puppies to give the mother dog ("She has spots and ears that flop down. So does this puppy.")

Note: Reproduce the puppies to use with the game on page 61.

Patterns for Sort the Puppies

Patterns for Sort the Puppies

Math Games and Centers EMC 735

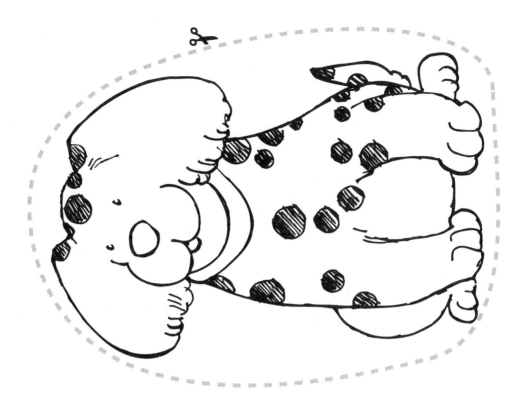

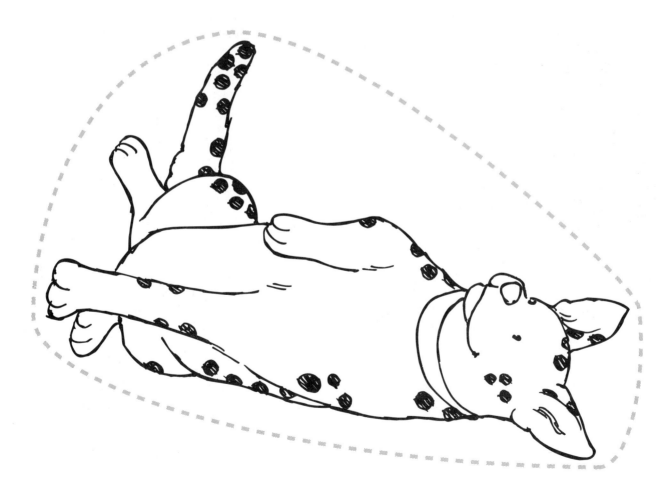

Note: Reproduce the dogs to use with the game on page 61.

Patterns for Sort the Puppies

Which Puppy Do You Like Best?

How to Make

1. Make a wall graph on a sheet of butcher paper (6' x 36" [2 m x 1 m]). Divide the paper into 6" (16.5 cm) columns. Draw a line 6" (16.5 cm) from the top.

2. Reproduce the puppies (see page 69 and 70). You will need one puppy for each of the six heading boxes.

3. Reproduce multiple copies of each puppy for students to select from.

How to Play

1. Have students sit around the graph.

2. Show each puppy and say its name. Have students repeat the names after you.

3. Have each child pick the dog they like best from the pictures you have provided.

4. Ask each child to name the dog chosen and glue or tape it on the graph. Child says, "I like beagles best. I am putting it in the beagle row."

5. When all students have placed their puppies on the graph, teacher asks questions such as:

   • What can we find out from this graph?

   • Which has the most? Which has the least?

   • Are there any rows (columns) that are the same? What does that tell us?

   • How many_____ are there?

   • Are there more (less) _____or_____?

Play with Beginners

Make a "yes-no" graph to answer the question "Do you have a pet dog?"

Write the question "Do you have a pet dog?" at the top of a sheet of chart paper. Divide the paper into two columns labeled "yes" and "no." Give each child a puppy cut out of construction paper (use one of the puppies from pages 69-70 as a pattern).

Take a puppy and place it on the graph to model the activity. Say "I put my dog under 'yes' because I have a dog." Then have each child come up and tape his/her puppy to the graph. Ask students to tell why they are putting their puppy in a certain column.

Note: Reproduce these puppies to use with the graph on page 67.   **Patterns for Which Puppy Do You Like Best?**

Corgi

Beagle

Cocker Spaniel

69

Note: Reproduce these puppies to use with the graph on page 67. **Patterns for Which Puppy Do You Like Best?**

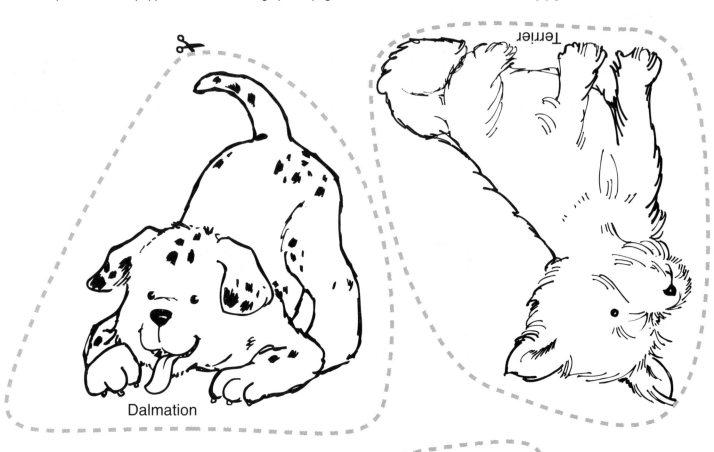

Terrier

Dalmation

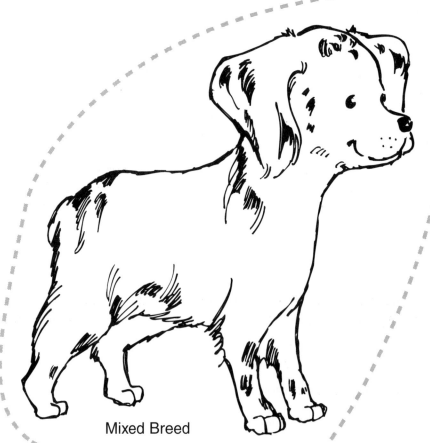

Mixed Breed

Follow the Puppy

How to Make

1. Reproduce the pawprints on page 73 on light brown construction paper or cut pawprints from tagboard. You will need one pawprint for each number you wish to practice.

2. Write a number on each pawprint.

3. Laminate and cut out the pawprints.

How to Play

1. Mix up the numbered pawprints and tape them in a line on the floor. (Match the distance between pawprints to the length of the students' steps.) Place a stuffed toy puppy at the end of the pawprints for students to "catch."

   Choose the numbers appropriate to the skill level and attention span of your students. Some will be ready for a short line of numbers 1-5. Others may be ready for a line of numbers from 1-20.

2. Students form a line behind the first pawprint.

3. The first child walks the pawprints, saying each number before it is stepped on, trying to get to the end without making a mistake. If a child does misname a number, either provide the correct number and let the child continue or say the number yourself and have the him/her return to the end of the line to try again.

   When a child gets to the end of the pawprints, he/she sits down to watch the next child in line.

Variation—Identifying Shapes

Reproduce pawprints. Glue a basic shape (see page 112) on each pawprint before laminating and cutting out. Students walk from one shape to the next, saying the name of the shape before stepping on it.

Advanced Play

Students say the shape name and give one of its characteristics (a circle is round; a circle doesn't have corners; etc.).

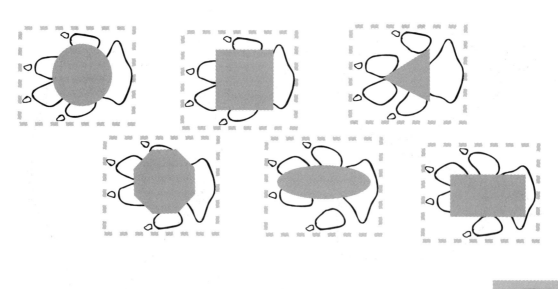

Patterns for Follow the Puppy

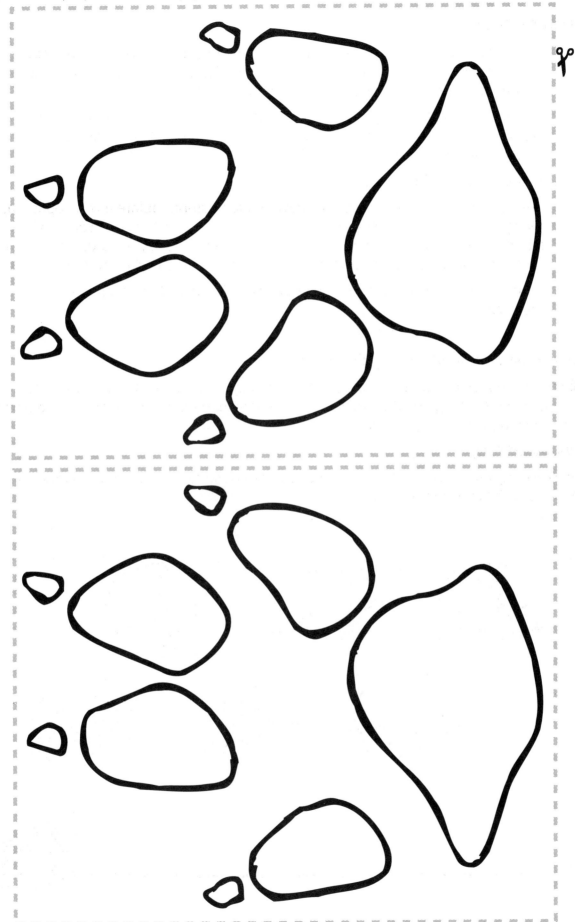

73

Puppies in a Row

How to Make

1. Reproduce the puppies on pages 69 and 70. (You will need one puppy for each number you are practicing.)

2. Write a number on each puppy.

3. Laminate and cut out the puppies.

Note: To play the variation on page 75, reproduce the puppies, but don't write numbers on them. Make each puppy different by coloring it or adding a collar, jacket, etc.

How to Play

1. Have students sit in a line facing the teacher. Give each child one or more puppies. Teacher keeps number "1."

2. Place puppy number one on the carpet. Say "This is number '1.' What comes next?" Ask the child with that number to place it after the one. Continue until all numbers are in order.

3. When all puppies have been put in a row, point to each puppy as students read its number. If a number is out of order ask for a volunteer to put it in the correct place and then read the numbers again.

Variation

Play Which Puppy Is First? to practice ordinal numbers.

Lay three or more puppies in a row. Ask students to tell which puppy is first in line. Remove that puppy and ask students to tell which puppy is first now. Ask which puppy is last. Remove that puppy and ask students to tell which puppy is last now.

Point to each puppy and count using ordinal numbers. Have students repeat after you. (First, second, third, etc.) Ask students to identify the third puppy. Repeat with each puppy in line.

Puppy Centers

• Feed the Puppies

Reproduce the puppy food dishes (see page 59). Write a number on each food dish. Reproduce several sets of bones. Laminate and cut out the dishes and bones. Put the bones in a bag labeled "Puppy Bones." The child's task is to read the number and put that many bones on the dish.

• Find My Puppies

Reproduce the mother dogs on pages 65 and 66 and the puppies on pages 63 and 64. Laminate and cut out the pieces. The child's task is to match each of the puppies to the correct mother.

• Puppy Patterns

Provide puppy patterning strips (see page 78) and a container of puppies (see page 77). The child's task is to copy each of the patterns.

Extend the activity for more advanced students by providing blank strips of tagboard, extra puppy patterns, and glue. The child creates a puppy pattern and then glues the pattern on a tagboard strip.

• Count My Spots

Reproduce the dalmatians on pages 79 and 80. Laminate and cut them out. The child's task is to count the dots on each puppy and put them in numerical order.

Extend the activity by having more advanced students build equations. Write +, -, and = signs on file cards. Students arrange the spotted puppies and cards to create an equation.

Patterns for Puppy Centers

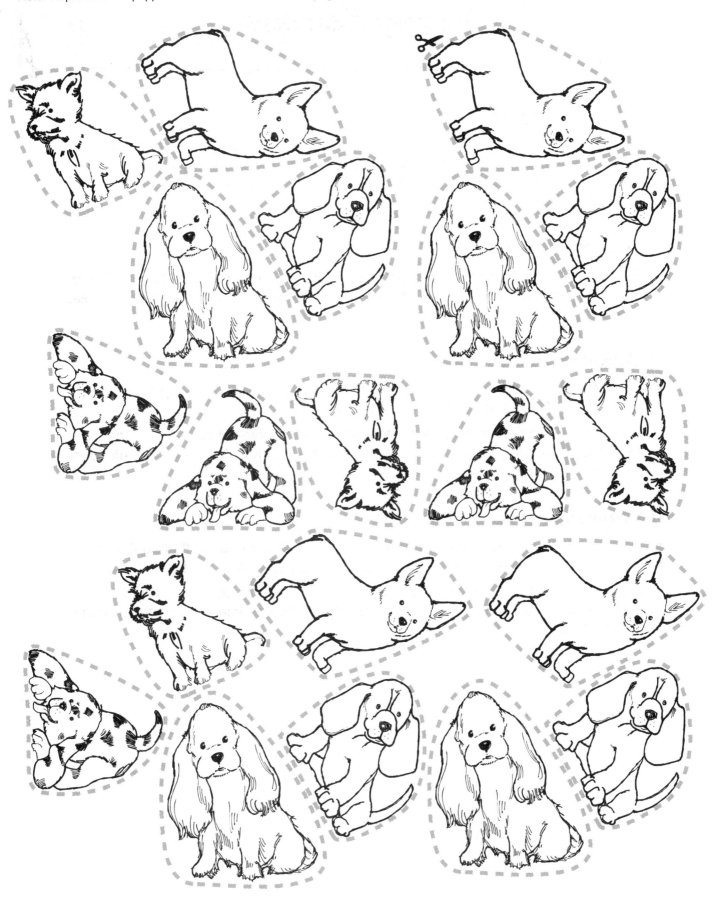

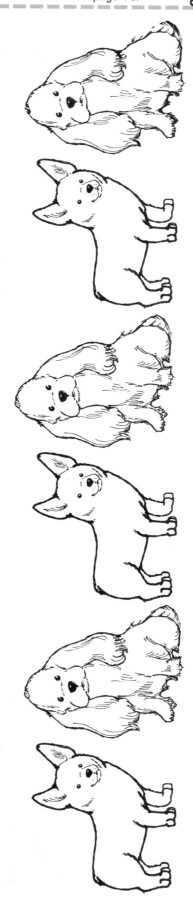
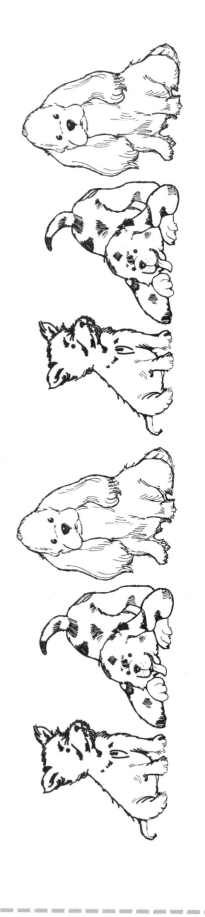

78

Patterns for Puppy Centers

Note: Reproduce the puppies to use with the game on page 76.

Patterns for Puppy Centers

How Many Mittens?

How to Make

You will need mittens in several sizes and colors (ask parents to contribute old pairs from home; try yard sales and thrift shops).

How to Play

1. Have students sit in a line facing the teacher. Teacher places several mittens in front of the students.

2. Call up one child. Ask "How many mittens do I need to give (child's name) ?" If students have difficulty coming up with an answer, have the child raise each hand as the group counts. Have the child take two mittens, put them on, and sit back in the line.

3. Continue play, calling up two, then three, etc. students each time. Follow the directions in step 2.

4. When all students have a pair of mittens ask "How many mittens do we need for everyone in the group?" Have students help you count as each child holds up their mittens.

Advanced Play—Pairs of Mittens

Explain that two mittens make up a pair. Play the game again asking "How many pairs of mittens do I need to give.....?"

Variations

Make a Pair

Reproduce the mittens on pages 84 - 87. Cut them out. Lay out the mittens containing numbers. Pass out the mittens containing sets of snowflakes. Students count the snowflakes on their mitten and match it to the correctly numbered mitten. When the match is made, have each child read the number aloud ("My mittens say 3.").

If you want to practice numbers greater than ten, reproduce the mitten forms on page 95 and write in your own numbers and pictures.

Mittens in a Row

Hang a piece of thick yarn between two chairs. Provide clothespins. Use the mittens containing numbers from Make a Pair.

Pass out the mittens and have students hang them in numerical order from the smallest to the largest number on the clothes line.

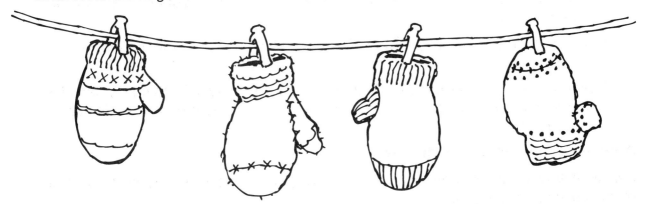

Advanced Play—Count By Twos

You will need five pairs of mittens and a set of cards containing the numbers 2, 4, 6, 8, and 10.

Have students sit in a circle. Place a pair of mittens in the center. Ask "How many mittens do you see?" After the answer is given, lay the number card 2 below the mittens. Place a second set of mittens next to the first. Ask "How many mittens do you see now?" After the answer is given, lay the number card 4 under the second pair of mittens. Continue with all five sets of mittens. Then explain that things that come in pairs can be counted by twos. Point to each number in order and say it with the students. Allow volunteers to read the numbers on their own.

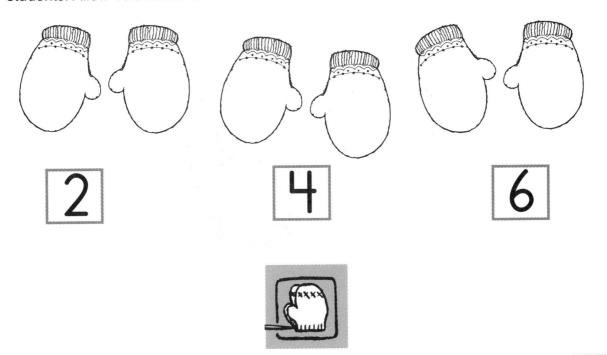

Note: Reproduce the mittens to use with the variation on page 82.

Patterns for How Many Mittens?

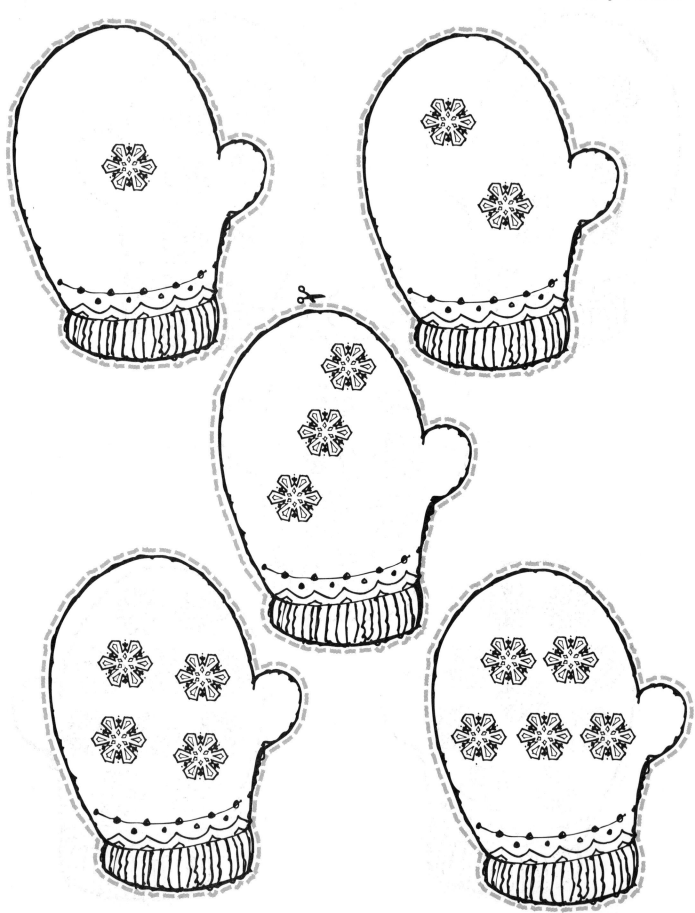

Math Games and Centers EMC 735

Note: Reproduce the mittens to use with the variation on page 82.

Patterns for How Many Mittens?

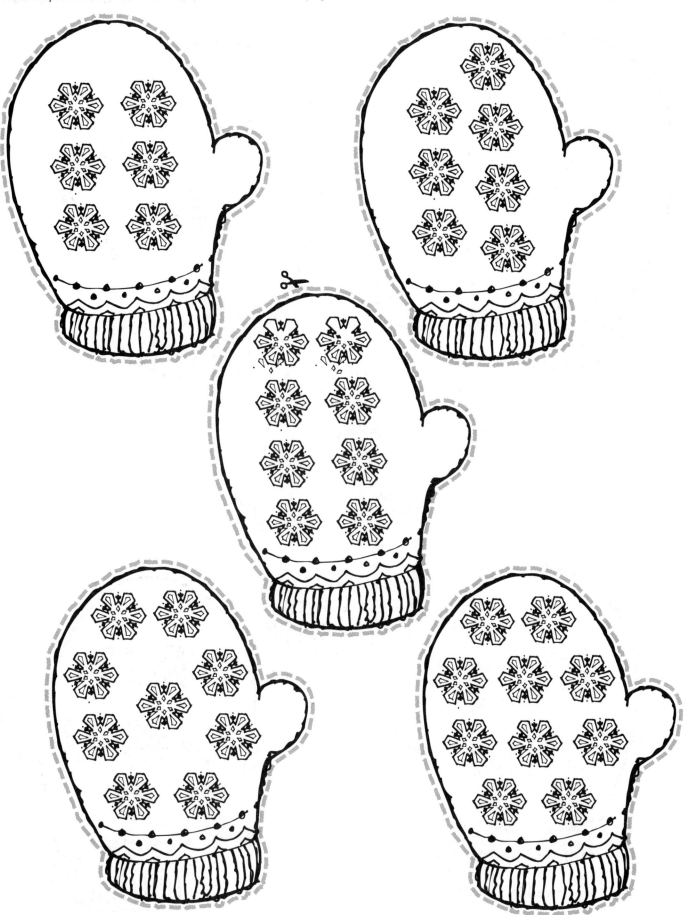

Note: Reproduce the mittens to use with the variation on page 82.

Patterns for How Many Mittens?

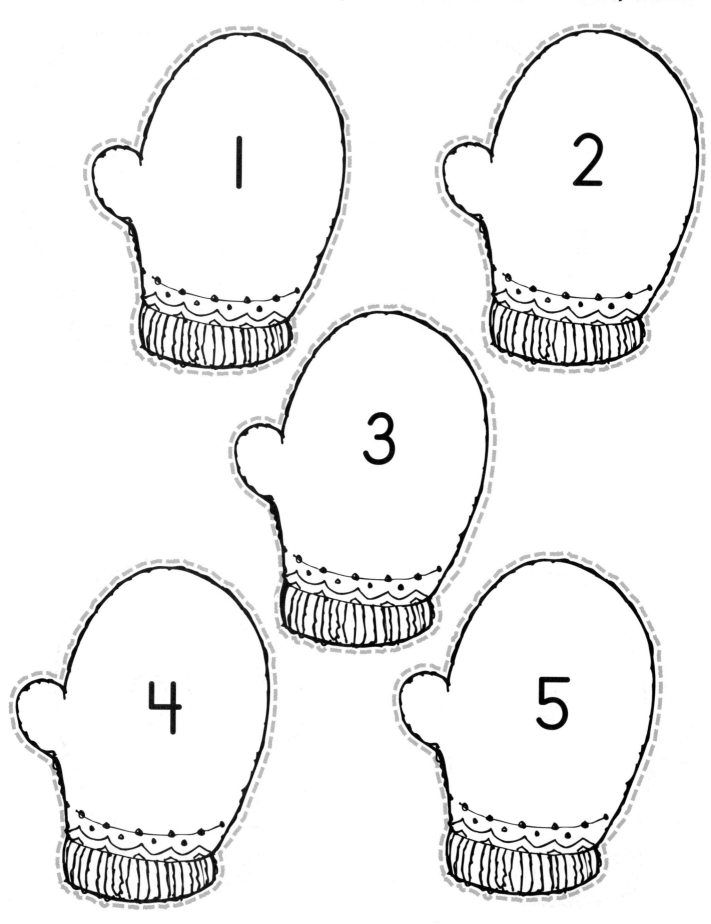

Note: Reproduce the mittens to use with the variation on page 82.

Patterns for How Many Mittens?

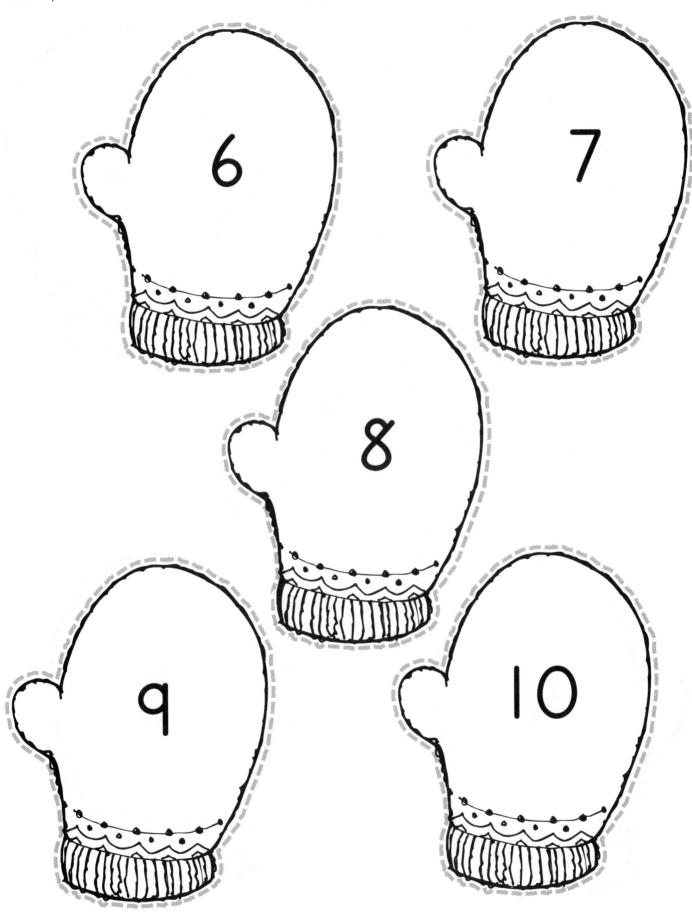

Math Games and Centers EMC 735

Make a Pair

How to Make

1. You will need several pairs of real mittens and some dolls or stuffed animals with "hands." Put one mitten from a pair on each animal (size doesn't matter).

2. Reproduce pages 90 and 91 for each player. Cut out the mittens and place one complete set in a self-locking plastic bag.

How to Play

1. Have students sit in a row facing the stuffed animals or dolls. Have them observe the mittens being worn.

2. Pass out a mitten to each child. Have the students find the mate to their mittens. Have them put the mitten on the stuffed animal or doll to show they have made their match.

3. Collect the mittens. Put them in a paper sack. Have each child take a mitten from the sack and then find their partner to make a pair.

4. Give each child a sorting sheet and a plastic bag of mittens. Students place the mittens in pairs on the hands.

Variation—Match the Mitten

Reproduce page 92 for each child. Students look at the design on the left mitten and then draw the same design on the right mitten. If your students are ready for more complicated designs, add greater detail before reproducing the form.

Note: Reproduce the sorting chart to use with the game on page 88.

Patterns for Make a Pair

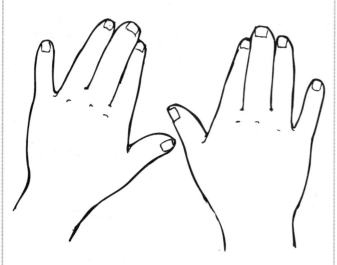

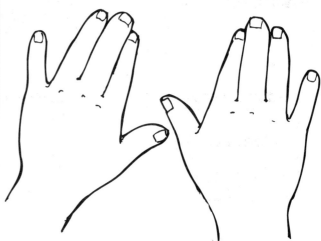

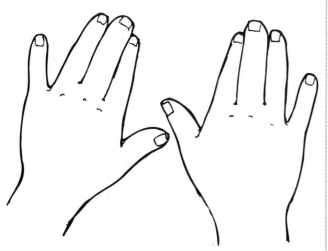

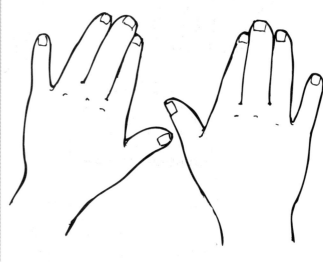

Pattern for Make a Pair

Note: Reproduce the form to use with the variation on page 88.

Patterns for Make a Pair

Do You Wear Mittens?

How to Make

1. Make a Yes-No Graph.

    a. Take a sheet of chart paper. Divide it as shown.

    b. Write "Do You Wear Mittens?" at the top.

    c. Write "yes" and "no" as headings.

2. Reproduce the mittens (one per child) on page 95. Cut them out.

How to Play

1. Have students sit facing the graph.

2. Pass out a mitten to each child. Remind students that you are asking them whether or not they wear mittens.

3. Have students decide whether their mitten goes in the "yes" or in the "no" column. Tape your own mitten on the graph as you say "I am putting my mitten under 'no' because I don't wear mittens." Have students come up, one at a time, to tape their mittens on the graph.

4. Ask questions such as:

    • How many people wear mittens?

    • How many people don't wear mittens?

    • Do more people wear mittens than don't wear them?

Variation — Do You Wear Mittens or Gloves?

Instead of "yes" and "no" use a mitten and a glove as headings for the graph. (Use a mitten pattern with lines drawn for finger spaces to use as a glove.)

Make enough gloves and mittens for each child playing the graphing game. Have each child select a mitten or a glove and tape it to the correct column on the graph. Have students who wear neither select the one they would prefer to wear.

Pattern for Do You Wear Mittens?

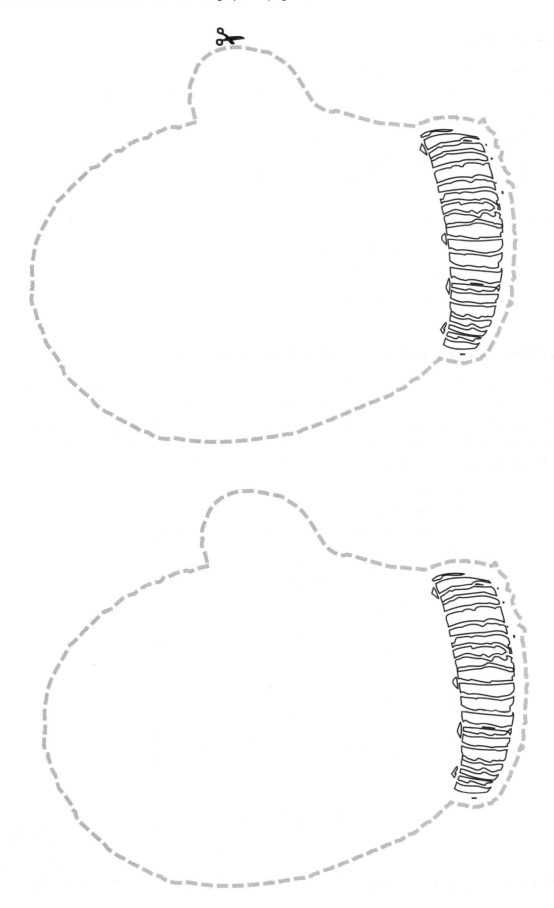

•Mitten Concentration

This is a center for two students at a time.

Mitten concentration can be played by matching snowflakes and numbers (pages 84-87) or matching numbers (two sets of pages 86 and 87).

Show students how to play concentration:

Place the mitten cards number-side down in two or three lines. The first student turns over two mittens saying the number on each. If the two numbers match the child takes the two mittens. If the numbers don't match, the mittens are turned back over in the same place. The other player takes a turn. Play continues until all of the mittens have been taken.

•Make a Pair

Reproduce the mittens on pages 97 and 98. Color, laminate, and cut apart the playing pieces. The child's task is to match a shape with a picture of an object with that shape.

•Hang the Mittens Out to Dry

Provide a collection of construction paper mittens. (Use pattern on page 95.) Use only colors or add simple designs to some of the mittens. Reproduce several of each type.

Attach a yarn clothesline to a bulletin board. Pin a pattern of mittens to the line.

Hang a second clothesline between two chairs. Sit the chair beneath the bulletin board clothesline. Provide mittens and clothespins. The child's task is to copy the pattern by hanging mittens on the line.

✂

Patterns for Mitten Centers

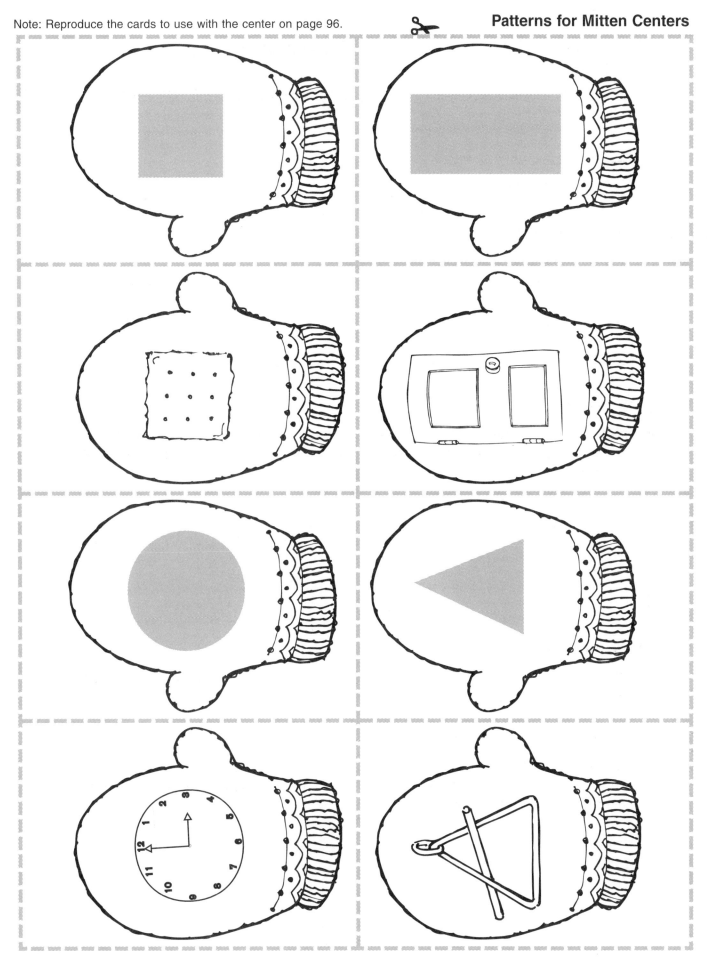

✁ **Patterns for Mitten Centers**

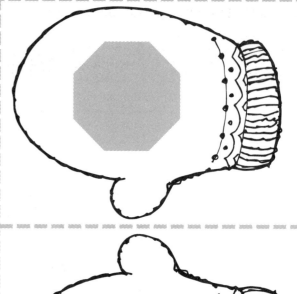

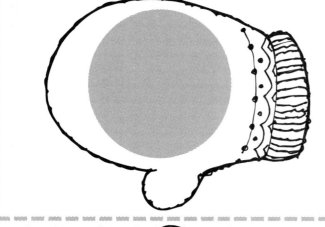

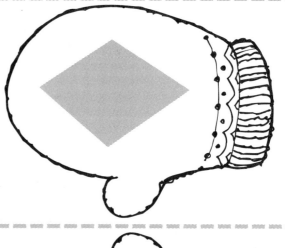

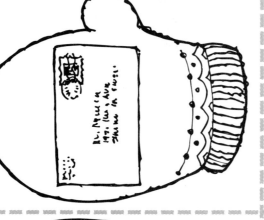

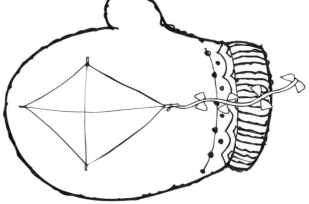

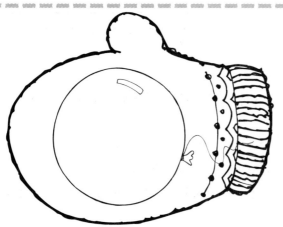

Feed the Elephant

Note: Use peanuts for games only with close adult supervision. If you feel using small items is not appropriate for your students, reproduce only the whole peanuts from the patterns on page 102.

How to Make

1. Reproduce the elephant counting card on page 101. You will need one card for each child.

2. Reproduce the number cards on the inside back cover.

3. Laminate and cut out the cards. Put the cards in a small sack.

4. Each child will need at least as many peanuts as the largest number they will be practicing.

How to Play

1. Have students sit in a circle. Give each child an elephant counting card and a set of peanuts.

2. Hand the sack to one child. He/She takes out a card and places it in the corner of the playing card. The sack is passed around so each child can pick a number.

3. Students read their number and "feed" that many peanuts to the elephant. Go around the circle, having each child tell how many peanuts were fed to the elephant. ("I fed six peanuts to my elephant.") If a child makes a mistake, have him/her touch each peanut and count in sequence to correct the answer.

4. Collect the number cards and pass the sack around again. Continue play.

Play with Beginners

Call a child to sit with you. The teacher places a number of peanuts on each counting card. The child counts the peanuts and puts the same amount on the card. (If the child is not yet counting independently, have him/her place a peanut below each one on the card, and then touch and count the peanuts with the adult.) Repeat this for each card.

Variation—How Many Peanuts in the Bag?

Take some small bags. Write a number (appropriate for your students) on each of the bags. Give one bag and a pile of peanuts to each child. They are to read the number and put that many peanuts in the bag.

Note: Reproduce the counting card to use with the game on page 99.

Pattern for Feed the Elephant

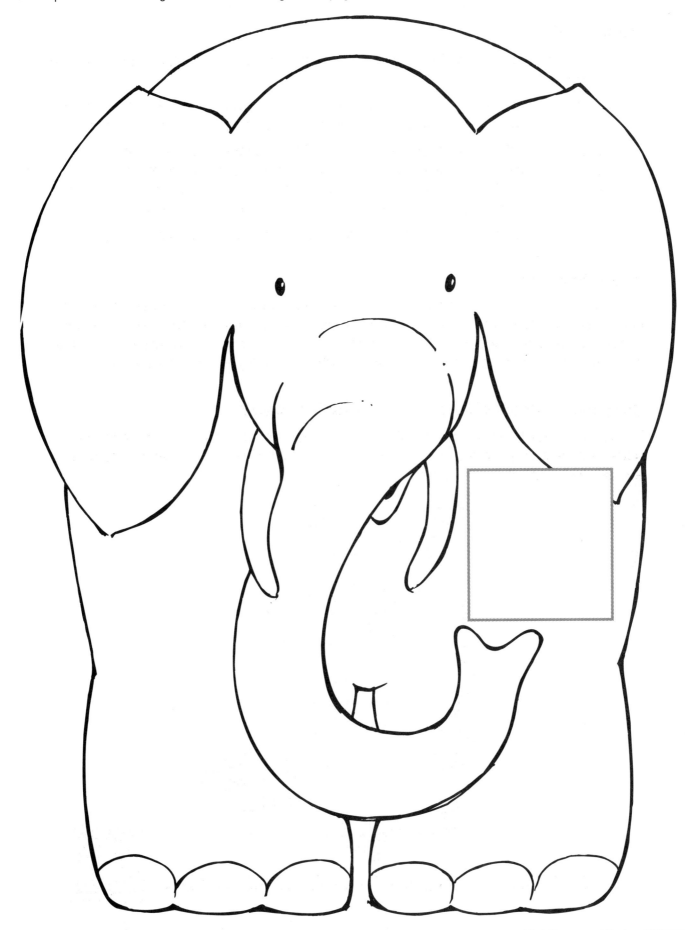

Note: Reproduce the peanut shapes to use with the game on page 99.

Peanut Patterns

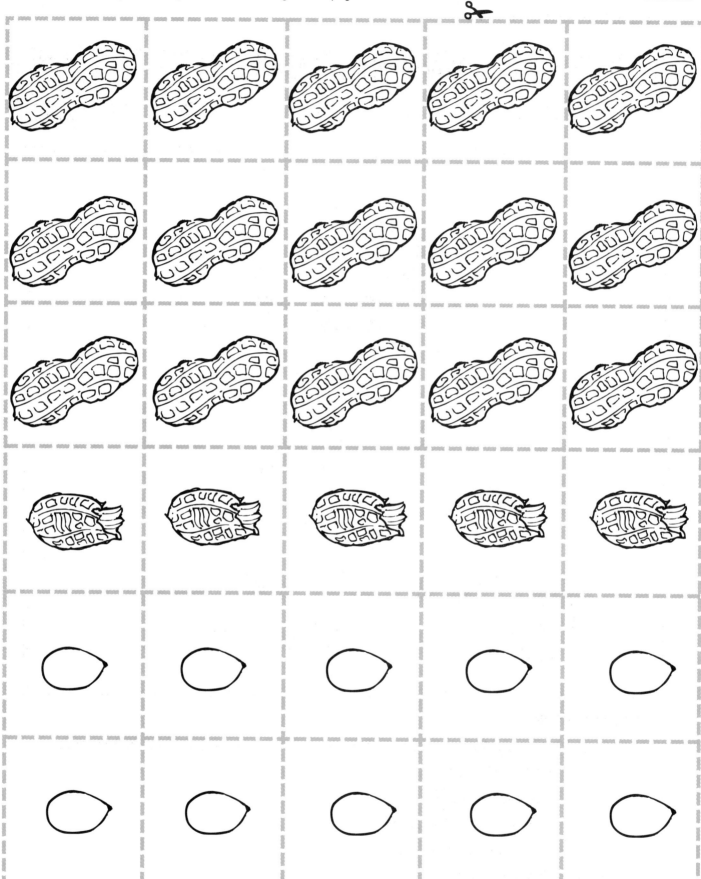

Sort the Shells

How to Make

1. You need a large bag of peanuts in the shell. Use those that fit these categories:
   - different sizes
   - stems/no stems
   - broken shells/whole shells
   - one nut/multiple nuts

2. Provide 2 small bowls.

3. Reproduce the sorting sheet on page 105.

Math Games and Centers EMC 735

How to Play

1. Students and teacher sit in a circle. Put two small bowls in the center of the circle.

2. Give each child two nuts of different sizes. The teacher places one larger nut in one bowl and one smaller nut in the other bowl. Ask students to sort their nuts in the same way.

   Examine the nuts in each bowl and have students decide if any are misplaced.

3. Give each child a small pile of peanuts—at least one with one nut, several with two nuts, and a copy of the sorting sheet. Ask students to sort their nuts into two piles on their sorting sheets.

   Have students work in pairs to check each other's piles to see if any nuts are misplaced.

4. Continue having students sort their peanuts according to different attributes (whole/broken, dark spots/no dark spots, etc.)

Advanced Play

Have students sort their nuts by two attributes.

- large and whole/large and broken
- small and whole/small and broken
- large and two nuts/large and one nut

Note: Reproduce the sorting card to use with the game on page 103.

Patterns for Sort the Shells

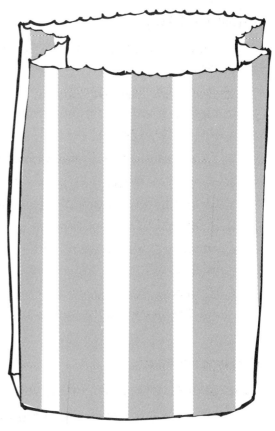

How Many Nuts Are in Your Shell?

How to Make

1. Make a four-column floor graph.

   a. Cut a 3-foot (1 meter) length of 24" (61 cm) wide butcher paper.

   b. Use a marking pen to divide the graph into 6" (16.5 cm) columns.

2. Make header cards.

   a. Fold four pieces of 6" by 12" tagboard in half. Glue one empty peanut shell (see page 108) on each header card.

   b. Write a number on each card and draw that number of peanuts in the shell.

3. Reproduce one peanut shell (see page 108) per student.

4. Provide a bag of peanuts.

How to Play

1. Have students sit in a circle around the floor graph.

2. Each student will need a real peanut and a peanut pattern.

3. Have students open their peanut and count out the nuts. Each child places his/her peanut pattern on the graph in the correct column saying "I have (two) peanuts in my shell."

4. When everyone has had a turn, ask questions about the graph.

    • How many peanuts' shells had three (two, one, no) nuts?

    • Which row has the most nuts?

    • Which row has the fewest nuts?

Variation

1. Make a wall graph on a sheet of butcher paper (36" x 36" [1 m x 1 m]). Divide the paper into 6" (16.5 cm) columns. Draw a line 6" (16. 5 cm) from the top.

2. Reproduce the empty peanut shell pattern on page 108. You will need one shell for each student and four shells for the heading boxes.

3. Write a number (0, 1, 2, 3) and glue an empty peanut shell in each heading box. Draw the appropriate number of nuts in each shell.

4. Give one real peanut and one empty shell pattern to each child. Have students open their peanuts, count the number of nuts it contains, and draw that many nuts on their shells.

5. Have each child tape or glue their peanuts in the correct column of the graph. Ask questions about the graph.

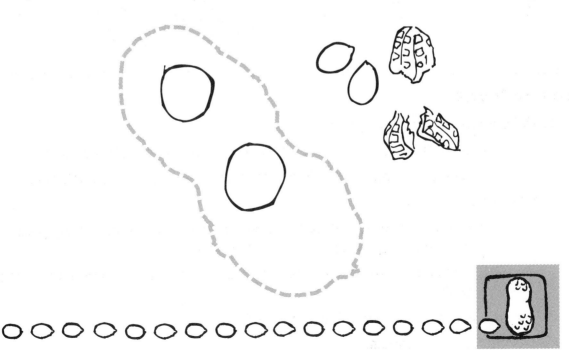

Note: Reproduce the peanut forms to use with the wall graph on page 106.

Patterns for How Many Nuts Are in Your Shell?

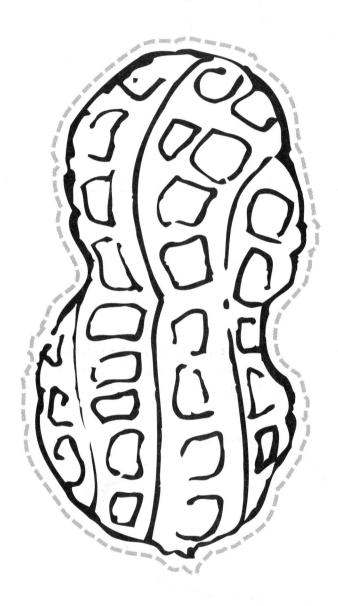

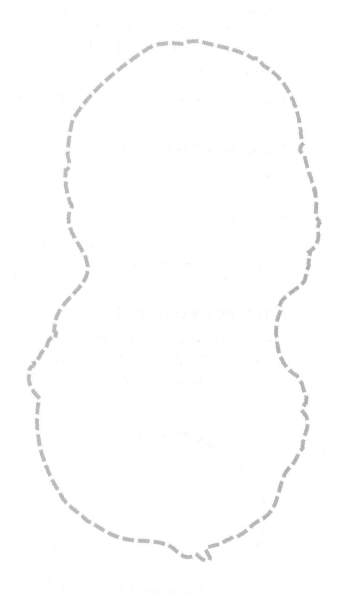

Math Games and Centers EMC 735

•Peanut Match

Reproduce and cut out the empty peanut shell pattern on page 108 (as many times as needed for the number of matches you desire). Cut peanuts (see pattern below) out of light brown construction paper. Write a number on one peanut and make a set of dots on the other peanut. The child's task is to put the matching peanuts in the same shell.

Advanced Play for Beginning Readers

Put number names on peanuts instead of dot patterns.

•Peanut Patterning

Reproduce copies of the peanuts on page 102 and the patterning cards on pages 110 and 111. The child's task is to copy the patterns.

Advanced Play

Provide blank strips of paper (4" x 12" [10 x 30.5 cm]). The child makes a pattern with peanuts and then glues it to the paper strip.

•Feed the Elephant

Reproduce an elephant card (see page 101) for each number you wish your students to practice. Write a number on each card. Provide a bag of peanuts (real or copies from page 102). The child's task is to read the number and to put that many nuts on the elephant.

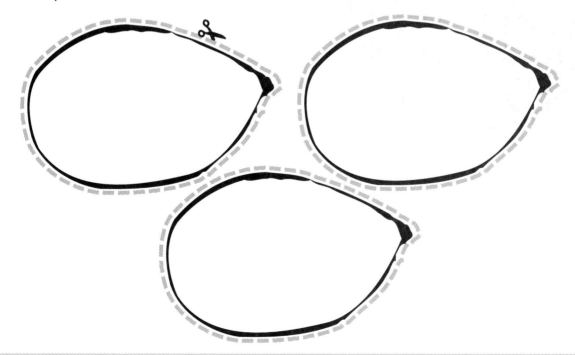

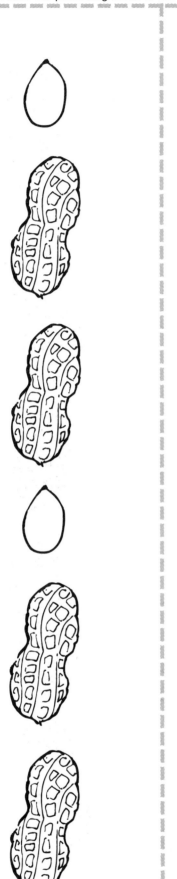

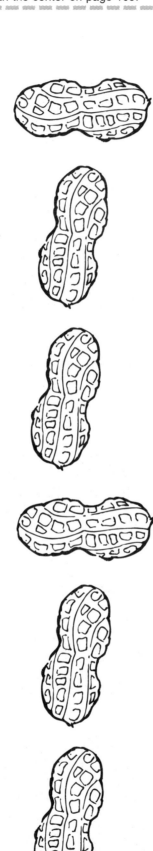

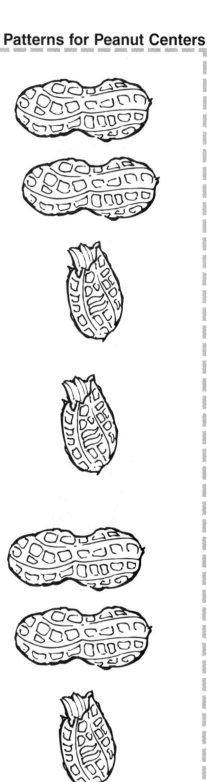

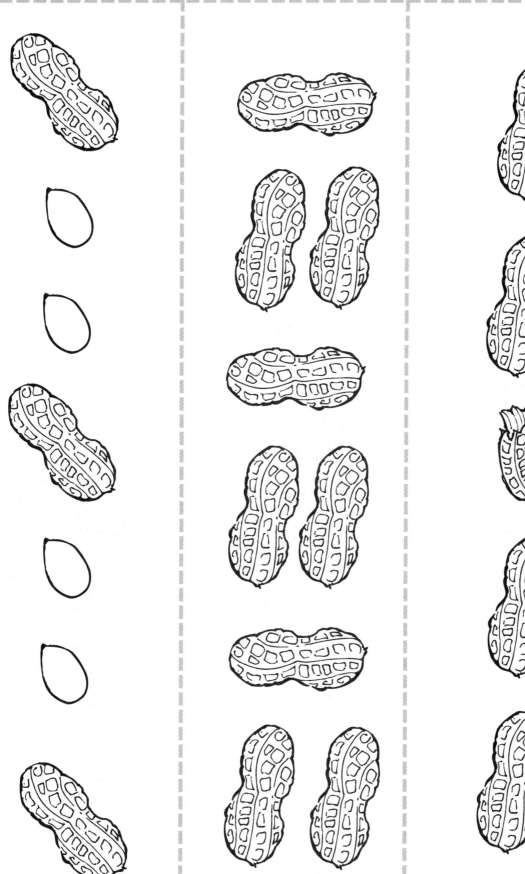

Note: Reproduce the shapes to use with the games on pages 32 and 72.

Geometric Shape Patterns